The Moulding of Communists

FRANK S. MEYER

THE MOULDING
OF COMMUNISTS

THE TRAINING OF
THE COMMUNIST CADRE

A HARVEST BOOK

Harcourt, Brace & World, Inc., New York

From The God That Failed, edited by Richard Crossman:

Selection by Arthur Koestler (pp. 45, 46, 47)—Copyright 1949 by Richard Crossman.

Selection by Richard Wright (pp. 154-57, with deletions) —Copyright 1944 by Richard Wright.

Reprinted by permission of Harper & Row, Publishers, and Hamish Hamilton Ltd.

This book is one of a series of studies of Communist influence in American life. The entire survey has been made possible through the foresight and generous support of the Fund for the Republic. All of us who have taken part in it are grateful for this exceptional opportunity to study the most confused and controversial problem of the age and to publish the results exactly as we find them.

CLINTON ROSSITER

CONTENTS

I   *The Communist in Focus* 3

Part One

THE THEORY OF COMMUNIST TRAINING

II   *The Mould* 9

THE IDEAL TYPE 10
THE ROLE OF THE CADRE 13
THE CHARACTERISTICS OF THE IDEAL TYPE 16
CYNICISM AND IDEALISM 24

III   *The Mechanism of Pressure: The Party* 27

FORMS OF PARTY TRAINING 28
METHODOLOGY OF PARTY TRAINING 32
"SCIENCE," CONTROL AND RESPONSIBILITY 38
PRESSURE 40
THE TRANSFORMATION OF THE TOTAL PERSONALITY 45

IV   *Philosophical Pressure: Marxism-Leninism* 49

A CLOSED MATERIAL UNIVERSE 52
LIFE AND THOUGHT AS CONTROL:
    THE UNITY OF THEORY AND PRACTICE 54
MORAL THEORY 56
HISTORICAL MATERIALISM 58
THEORY OF THE PARTY 61
ECONOMIC THEORY 63
THEORY OF THE STATE 66
STRATEGY AND TACTICS 69

V   *Psychological Pressure* 72

THE THEORY OF PERSONALITY—
    A DIALECTICAL DRAMA 75
REDUCTIONISM 78
COMMUNIST PSYCHOSURGERY 80

ix

Part Two
THE PRACTICE OF COMMUNIST TRAINING

VI   *Recruits* 89

       THE OBJECTIVE FACTORS 90
       THE SUBJECTIVE FACTORS 93
       RECRUITMENT PROPER 95
       TECHNIQUES OF RECRUITMENT 96

VII   *The Rank and File* 104

       THE NEW MEMBER 105
       NEW MEMBERS' CLASSES 111
       THE RANK AND FILER 114
       THE PARTY MEETING 114
       THE ACTIVITIES OF THE RANK-AND-FILE
          PARTY MEMBER 122
       THE IMPACT OF THE PARTY IN DAILY LIFE 125

VIII   *The Cadre* 132

       THE CADRE CRISIS 133
       TRANSITION TO THE CADRE 142
       TRAINING IN THE LIFE OF THE CADRE 144
       "SELF-CRITICISM," "SUBJECTIVITY," "OBJECTIVITY" 152

IX   *Party Training Schools* 159

       RANK-AND-FILE SCHOOLS AND CLASSES 160
       THE CADRE SCHOOLS 161
       SELECTION OF STUDENTS 162
       FUNCTION OF THE SCHOOLS 163
       CURRICULUM 165

       Conclusion 170

       Acknowledgments 175

       Notes 177

       Index 210

The Moulding of Communists

ONE · THE COMMUNIST IN FOCUS

This book is an attempt to depict as objectively as possible the process whereby the Communist man is created. At the same time, it is in a certain sense subjective, for it represents the conclusions of a large sector of a lifetime spent in acceptance, rejection, and examination of Communism. It reflects fourteen years of active leadership, theoretical and practical, in the Communist movement, followed by fifteen years of reorientation and deep consideration of this modern tyranny over the human mind and spirit.

An understanding of a movement of cardinal historical effect would seem to require a grasp of its ethos, of the fundamental dynamic which inspires and guides the individuals who compose it. Without such a grasp—such an apprehension from within, as it were—the most extensive analysis in terms of behavior, or of social cause and effect, will fail to present the living dimension of the movement. This is true whether the subject of study is an event in the past, where the mode of inquiry is historical, or in the present, where it is, broadly speaking, sociological; whether it is a phenomenon which expresses and reinforces our ideals and aspirations or one which is inimical to them.

It is in this sense that the commonplace "to fight Communism, we must understand it" is profoundly true. But only in this sense. The fight against Communism is not benefited by the kind of "understanding" which insists on reducing the reality to categories with which we are comfortably familiar. That way we misread both the range of human nature and the potentialities of Communism for evil. Rather, the imaginative effort must be made to apprehend the profoundly different character of Communist consciousness—different from anything with which we are acquainted.

For the Communist *is* different. He thinks differently. Reality looks different to him. He is not simply—and this is where many painstaking analyses go wrong—a mirror image of ourselves, with our motivations, ordinary or neurotic, hidden under a net of rationalizations couched in barbarous Hegelianisms and Russianisms.

Though different, however, the Communist consciousness can be and constantly is created anew through the transformation of normal non-Communist consciousness, a transformation purposively carried through in the training process that moulds the Communist cadre. It is the aim of this book to describe that process and thus help the reader make the imaginative leap necessary to grasp what the cadre Communist is, what his consciousness is like, and how he sees the world.

It is the cadre with which this book is concerned. The cadre is that core within the formal Communist Parties which represents Lenin's "organization of professional revolutionaries." Obviously, millions come into contact with Communist ideas, and hundreds of thousands are recruited to the parties and spend a greater or less period of time therein as rank and filers, without ever becoming Communists in the full sense. If I touch upon the process of recruiting from the world outside into the Communist Party, or upon the life and training of the recruit and of the rank and filer, that is only because the cadre man was once a non-Communist, a recruit, and a rank and filer, and because all these stages are part of the history of his development. The moulding process which transforms the personality and creates the full Communist begins at the first moment of contact with the penumbra of Communist influence, and continues with greater and greater intensity through each stage.

In the consideration of the cadre itself, I have further narrowed the focus and have concentrated my attention upon the process whereby the personality and outlook of the Communist are created. Communist organization, Party functioning, and strategy and tactics are considered only to the degree that they are directly relevant to that process. They are significant only insofar as they are at the disposal of Communist will; and that will is a function of a particular kind of person, the Communist person.

My experience covers only a decade and a half of the four decades in which Communism has been a world-wide movement and only a few countries of the West directly; but every indication from that experience and from the experience of others digested in the massive written record convinces me that (despite changes in the historical situation, despite differences of nation, even of civilization, despite the contrasting missions of Communists in power and out of power) a common secular and messianic quasi-religion inspires the Communist everywhere and from the beginning of the Communist movement till this day.

It is with the formation, the moulding, of the man who lives inspired by this outlook that this book deals. To understand him, what he is, what his goals are, what the continuing direction of his action is beneath the kaleidoscopic changes of strategy and tactics, is of the most vital importance to the West. Whether for the moment the Communist presents to the outer world the grim visage of overbearing ultimatum or the persuasive smile of coexistence, the inner purpose of Communism, the inner devotion of the Communist perseveres towards a consistent end.

PART ONE

•

THE
THEORY
OF
COMMUNIST
TRAINING

TWO · THE MOULD

Archimedes is reputed to have said: "But give me a fulcrum and I can move the world." Lenin's central idea was: Give me an organization of professional revolutionaries and I can transform the world. The Communist Party, the realization of the Leninist concept of an "organization of professional revolutionaries," is a fusion of three elements—doctrine, organization, people.

To speak of "people" as a factor coördinate with doctrine and organization, in discussing the elements of a party, an organization, an association, may seem rather strange. When we think of associations as such, those who compose them are not normally regarded as a factor of this kind, but rather taken for granted, as, in discussing the psychological makeup of a human being, his molecular constituents are taken for granted. But Communists do speak of "people" as a factor of this sort. In a passage which has the highest of authority in Communist discourse, Dmitrov writes: ". . . our Parties have not yet realized by far that *people, cadres, decide everything*. They are unable to do what Comrade Stalin taught us to do, namely, cultivate

cadres 'as a gardener cultivates his favorite fruit tree' . . ." [1]
(Emphasis in original).

"People" are conceived of, not as those who make up the
association, those for whom the association exists, but rather as
material to be developed, fertilized, watered—and pruned. It
may appear fantasy on my part to say that I have observed that
a special pitch and a special intonation accompany the use of
the world "people" in the Communist movement, but I think it
is so. At any rate, the written material proves by the words inter-
changeable with "people" that it has a very different connotation than in ordinary English. In place of it can be substituted
"forces," "elements," "material," "cadres" (used ungrammat-
ically as the plural of a hypothetical singular, "a cadre" or single
member of the cadre of the Communist movement).

"People" are "our people" [2]—another Communist phrase.
Communists in this sense, those who compose the core of the
movement, are very literally "our people." *They are made, not
born.* The Communist sympathizer, the new recruit to the Communist Party, even the Communist yearling, is still as a human
being much nearer to the character structure and the outlook of
the ordinary citizens from whose ranks he comes than he is to
the developed and seasoned Communists who make up the core,
the cadre, of the Party. These are the product of a continuing
process of training, of moulding, which creates them out of the
human material which comes to hand. [3]

THE IDEAL TYPE

To show how the developed Communist is thus moulded by the
conscious efforts of the Communist leadership is the aim of this

study. The mould in this process is an ideal type—the type of
the imagined perfect Communist, the bolshevik.

As in all human endeavor, that ideal type is never fully realized, even though there are within the Communist movement
historical and fictional persons who are presented as realiza-
tions of it. Men approach it approximately, and it is the meaning
of their existence and the aim of the Party that they approximate
it more and more closely. The honorific word, one spoken in this
sense with bated and admiring breath, is "bolshevik." No higher
praise exists in the Communist movement than to say of a person: "He's a real bolshevik." The image is emotionally deep-
ened by such oft-quoted slogans as "there are no obstacles that
bolsheviks cannot overcome," by the words of songs such as
that sung by the German Communists to the tune of Mussolini's
Giovinezza: "Bolshevisten, Bolshevisten, edelesten des Kom-
munisten."

Nor is this image merely a construction for the edification and
inspiration of the rank and file. It is a living and operative factor
in the lives of the cadre. It is drawn upon in training schools,
disciplinary sessions, inner-Party struggles. It is the vision
which fortifies men against prison and torture *and* against their
own inner revulsion when they accept or participate in frightful
atrocities or unprincipled deceptions.

The process, however, which moulds men to this single image
must begin with ordinary human beings in all their variety. The
raw material—Communist sympathizers and neophyte members
of the Party—includes psychological types of almost every kind.
While it is true that certain temperamental constitutions seem
better able to *survive* the process of conditioning, and these are
therefore represented to a greater degree among the cadre, the
differential seems to have much less to do with psychological type

than with something which, for want of a better word, I would call nervous toughness.

Since the ideal type is never fully realized, the differences between individuals, which continue to exist at every stage of approximation to the ideal, are dependent upon the original personality structure before the moulding. But while these differences are highly significant from the point of view of the psychologist and would be of great importance in the study of any single Communist as a human being, they are largely immaterial to the student of the Communist movement,[4] and in Communist practice itself are almost entirely disregarded. The important point is the degree of approximation to the ideal type. It is on this basis that leading Communists are selected for position, promoted, demoted, disciplined, and expelled. It is by this standard also that they judge themselves, regulate their lives, and are judged by their immediate associates. In fact, it is just to the degree that individual psychological traits remain that the Communist falls short of being a bolshevik.

In that most important tool of Communist training, "criticism and self-criticism," the most common critique of character is the accusation of "subjectivity." "Subjectivity" can take many forms, and each of these forms reflects a different original psychological characteristic of the individual. In all its forms, however, the same phenomenon is expressed: a failure of some sort in the process of replacing the motivations of the specific personal psychological type with the motivations of the ideal Communist type.

The significance of differences of psychological type is mainly negative. In the clash between the instinct of the personality for self-preservation and the moulding process seeking to make it over will be found one of the important causes of every break of a seasoned Communist with the movement. It is undoubtedly the main explanation also of a cycle of political breakdown and rehabilitation, which is the almost universal mark of the career of a long-time Communist.

Insofar as there is no perfect Communist, then, there do exist, as it were in suspension, many different types. But there are not a number of *Communist* types. There is one Communist type, more or less successfully dominating a series of original personality structures. For a study of the Communist as Communist, what is significant is this ideal type, the approximations to it, and the process of creating them.

THE ROLE OF THE CADRE

The men who approach the ideal type, Communists in the full sense, constitute a distinct body within the Communist movement. Before proceeding to a consideration of the characteristics of that type, their function and position must be delimited. The Communist movement as a whole includes members of the Party from top to bottom, close sympathizers of the Party, espionage and collateral underground agents inside or outside the formal Party organization. Actually possessing a Party card or functioning in an organizational unit of the Party (despite Lenin's dictum) is immaterial from any realistic point of view. The important criterion is acceptance of Communist discipline and directives. In this multitude of interconnecting and intricately correlated groupings, there exists a distinct élite, the members of which are recognizable by no title; who may or may not be in positions of organizational leadership; who in some cases may not, as a matter of fact, be formal card-holding members of the Communist Party. It is they who form what the Communists call the cadre.[5]

The word "cadre" is derived, of course, from military terminology, where it signifies the men who make up the frame, the skeleton of an existing or potential unit. Sometimes it also means the battle-hardened and experienced troops around whom a mass force can be developed. In Communist usage it is much nearer to this latter sense, but it has a specific meaning different from either.[6]

This élite, the Communist cadre, despite its lack of a formal organization, even of a formal existence, is the form taken in the course of the history of the Communist movement by Lenin's dream of an "organization of professional revolutionaries." The Communist Parties themselves are supposed to be the expression of that concept; but, owing to the large numbers admitted to their ranks, first in the Soviet Union, then in other countries where a policy of "mass parties" was adopted in the circumstances of Stalin's struggle for power, they ceased to fulfill that function. Hundreds of thousands within their ranks are in no real sense Communists, and many who are technically non-members are in the fullest sense Communists.

It is the cadre which has assumed the role assigned by Marxism-Leninism to "the Party." It is the cadre which is the "vanguard of the proletariat." It is the cadre which is "the only organization capable of centralising the leadership of the struggle of the proletariat, thus transforming each and every non-Party organization of the working class into an auxiliary body and transmission belt linking the Party with the class." [7] These words of Stalin's were spoken of the Party, not of the cadre, but the official Parties themselves have become hardly more than the most important of the mass organizations, master "transmission belts," schools and proving-grounds for the training of real Communists. (With the development of the institution of the cadre, the real reference of theoretical, inspirational, and practical statements on "the Party" is to the cadre, which is the soul of the Party.)

The cadre is not the formal leadership of the Communist movement. Most of the leaders, of course, are members of the cadre, although some may not be. Cadre Communists can be found in apparently the humblest of positions when there is reason for their activities at that level. An ostensible rank-and-file member may turn out to have associations, and to be performing functions, of the utmost importance, which prove him to be an accepted and trusted member of the inner core. Nor is the implication conveyed by a number of contemporary books about Communism true, that all espionage and underground personnel are of the cadre. The cadre directs and gives firmness to such work, as to all Communist work. But a dramatic spy or a policy-subverter in a high government post, a world-renowned writer or speaker or a Communist trade-union leader with great public prestige and power, may be little more than an office boy to obscure and unknown men with no *formal* position in or out of the Communist Party.[8]

The question remains: if the cadre has no official existence, how can it be identified and what is the source of its being? Members of the cadre are members of the cadre when they are recognized as such by their equals and superiors in the cadre. They become members of the cadre and achieve their status within the cadre by the decision of their superiors in the cadre; and the status of their superiors depends upon *their* superiors, etc. "Great fleas have little fleas upon their backs to bite 'em, And little fleas have lesser fleas, and so *ad infinitum*"—except that in this case we have not yet reached 1984. The infinite regress is cut short in the Political Bureau of the Communist Party of the Soviet Union, or in the person or persons who, at any time, possess the ultimate power within that organ.

The Communist in the full sense, the subject of this study, is the accepted member of the cadre. His development is continuous and never finished, but he is a Communist in contrast to other members of the Party, who are at most candidate-Communists. He is the "cadre Communist," the man who has been transformed to a greater or less degree into the ideal type.

THE CHARACTERISTICS OF THE IDEAL TYPE

The ideal type of the Communist is a man in whom all individual, emotional, and unconscious elements have been reduced to a minimum and subjected to the control of an iron will, informed by a supple intellect. That intellect is totally at the service of a single and compelling idea, made incarnate in the Communist Party: the concept of History as an inexorable god whose ways are revealed "scientifically" through the doctrine and method of Marxism-Leninism.

Such a vision of reality gives its possessor a tremendous feeling of power and of a certain kind of freedom, the "freedom" which, in Hegel's phrase, "is the recognition of necessity." "Ducunt Fata volentem, nolentem trahunt"—or, in a free Communist translation, "History inspires those who follow her willingly; those who do not are dragged by the tail or destroyed." [9] The servitors of History and the guardians of the lore of Marxism-Leninism are the initiate, the cadre, who constitute a quasi-priestly caste leading the potentially elect, the working class, to its apotheosis. There is a remarkable passage in Stalin's speech at the time of Lenin's death, a speech which is used as a sort of peroration in the Party schools and on solemn occasions. It conveys something of the intoxicating conviction of a special calling, which characterizes the Communist's attitude of devotion to the Party.

> We Communists are people of a special mould. We are made of special material. We are those who comprise the army of the great proletarian strategist, the army of Comrade Lenin. There is nothing higher than the honour to belong to this army. There is nothing higher than the title of member of the Party founded and led by Comrade Lenin. It is not given to all to be members of such a Party. It is not given to all to withstand the stress and storm that accompanies membership in such a Party. . . .
>
> In departing from us, Comrade Lenin bequeathed to us the duty of holding aloft and guarding the purity of the great title of member of the Party. We vow to you, Comrade Lenin, that we will fulfill your bequest with honour.[10]

Devotion. This is the first criterion for a cadre Communist.

> What shall be our *main criteria* in selecting cadres?
>
> First, *absolute devotion* to the cause of the working class, *loyalty to the Party,* tested in face of the enemy—in battle, in prison, in court.[11] (Emphasis in original.)

It is devotion, but devotion of a special kind. Neither this word nor the characterization "quasi-priestly" should make one lose sight of a fundamental difference between the Communist attitude and religious attitudes. What is intrinsic to the religious outlook—piety, humility, love—is missing from the Communist outlook. The essence of the devotion is control—control over nature, over man. In the technical sense, "magical," as contrasted with "religious," is the apt word, if by "magical" we mean the drive for power over fundamental forces through grasp of their character, and by "religious" we mean acceptance and love of God and man. In the outlook of the Communist man— in his dialectical materialist philosophy as in his Marxist-Leninist political theory, in his ethics and his aesthetics as in his personal inner life—those elements of existence which do not fall under the broad rubric of "change the world" quite literally do not exist. They are delusory shadows, totally derivative from the real, meaningful elements of existence. To argue the autonomous existence of joy, awe, aesthetic form, beauty, the satisfaction of intellectual curiosity is to play with meaningless questions, to lose one's way, bemused by the Siren voices of mocking phantoms rising from the decay of class society.

The ability to exercise this control is to be achieved strictly through the development of the rational conscious understanding. It is not that Communists are unaware of the existence of depths in the human personality, nor that they are unequipped with a theory and practice of psychological manipulation, but for themselves, for the élite, who are the forerunners of the "man of a new type," those depths are to be destroyed or brought under the most iron control of the consciousness.

For the Communist, therefore, the emphasis is overwhelmingly on the rational, interpreted in the light of Marxism-Leninism. In a Hegelian sense, "all that is real is rational" and "all that is rational is real."

The "Conclusion" of the *History of the Communist Party of the Soviet Union,* for long the leading Communist textbook of Marxism-Leninism, reads:

What are the chief conclusions to be drawn from the historical path traversed by the Bolshevik Party?

What does the history of the C.P.S.U.(B.) teach us? . . .

. . . The history of the Party . . . teaches us that a party of the working class cannot perform the role of leader of its class, cannot perform the role of organizer and leader of the proletarian revolution, unless it has mastered the advanced theory of the working-class movement, the Marxist-Leninist theory.

The power of the Marxist-Leninist theory lies in the fact that it enables the Party to find the right orientation in any situation, to understand the inner connection of current events, to foresee their course and to perceive not only how and in what direction they are developing in the present, but how and in what direction they are bound to develop in the future.

Only a party which has mastered the Marxist-Leninist theory can confidently advance and lead the working class forward.

On the other hand, a party which has not mastered the Marxist-Leninist theory is compelled to grope its way, loses confidence in its actions and is unable to lead the working class forward. . . .

The Marxist-Leninist theory is not a dogma but a guide to action.[12]

Or, in Dmitrov's words:

We Communists are people of action. Ours is the problem of practical struggle against the offensive of capital, against fascism and the threat of imperialist war, the struggle for the overthrow of capitalism. It is precisely this *practical* task that imposes upon the Communist cadres the obligation to equip themselves with *revolutionary theory*. For, as Stalin, that greatest master of revolutionary action, has taught us, theory gives those engaged in practical work the power of orientation, clarity of vision, assurance in work, confidence in the triumph of our cause.

But real revolutionary theory is irreconcilably hostile to any emasculated theorizing, any futile toying with abstract definitions. *Our theory is not a dogma, but a guide to action,* Lenin used to say. It is *such* theory that our cadres need, and they need it as badly as they need their daily bread, as they need air, water.[13] (Emphasis in original.)

It will be necessary in a later chapter to discuss at greater length the peculiar and integral meaning of "theory" for the Communist—a meaning profoundly different from that held either by the older rationalist tradition of the West or by the dominant anti-theoretical pragmatic-positivist outlook of our times. Marxist theory is a living ever-present mode of the personality. The outside observer might consider that the slogan "Without revolutionary theory there can be no revolutionary practice" is simply the utilization of doctrine to serve political policies. But, as it is understood by Communists together with its companion slogan, "unity of theory and practice," it has much deeper significance. However refined the dialectical explanation, the concept of "unity of theory and practice" always retains a residual content which, in the power and indeterminate quality of its impact, can only be described as mystical.

The compelling force of this idea makes possible the existence side by side in the Communist of two qualities which would appear to be fundamentally contradictory.

Dmitrov demands of the cadre:

. . . *ability independently to find one's bearings* and not to be afraid of *assuming responsibility in taking decisions.* He who fears to take responsibility is not a leader. He who is unable to display initiative, who says, "I will do only what I am told," is not a Bolshevik.[14] (Emphasis in original.)

And then:

. . . *discipline* and *Bolshevik hardening* in the struggle against the class enemy as well as in their irreconcilable opposition to all deviations from the Bolshevik line.[15] (Emphasis in original.)

How can a man be disciplined in the bolshevik manner, that is, how can he accept every brutal twist of the line, subordinate his moral and intellectual judgment absolutely to his superiors, call black white and white black between yesterday and today, and still retain "ability independently to find . . . [his] bearings and not . . . be afraid of assuming responsibility in taking decisions"?

It is obvious that it is impossible for a human being to be responsible, to have initiative and independence of judgment,

without a subjective feeling of being free. Acceptance of "bolshevik discipline"—with all the ramifications which the history
of recent years has shown that phrase to have—would seem,
therefore, to be possible only for one in whom such a feeling of
freedom had ceased to exist. But the unity of theory and practice enables the Communist to identify every act of the organization, even the most wanton exercise of authority over himself,
as a necessity of History. His theoretical outlook enables him to
"recognize" that necessity. To recognize it is to be free. And
this is not a matter of verbal gymnastics. It is simply the closest
I can get to expressing in explicit terms the inner rationale which
makes it possible for a feeling of independence and the actuality
of subservience to exist side by side.

It is this, I think, which explains much of the conduct of the
accused in the state trials of the Soviet Union.[16] They accepted
not only death, which many brave men have faced for their
ideals, but self-denigration, destruction of their very reputation
among men, to sustain a despised policy and a despised leader,
whom History had willed to be for the time the only possible
executor of its designs. This is the disciplined bolshevik personality exhibited in its most dramatic form. But in a thousand
small incidents, beginning with the first days of advancement to
the cadre, the attitude is inculcated and fostered. All Party experience and all Party training, theoretical and practical, lead
towards absolute and uncompromising acceptance of the decisions of the organization—not only in the face of prison, torture,
and death, but in the face of what were yesterday one's firmest
convictions. What is demanded is more than acceptance, more
than the carrying out of decisions. One must make those decisions one's own—even though one still knows that they are
wrong. A veteran of the Communist International once said to
me, talking of old inner-Party struggles and referring to the de-

feat of the Bukharinite Right opposition, of which he had himself been a leader: "Of course we were right—but the Party is always right."

Independence of judgment, ability and willingness to take responsibility and make decisions, are qualities which need comparatively little discussion. The words and phrases are straightforward and clear. One aspect, however, should be stressed—the almost unlimited versatility assumed in the ideal Communist. Marxism-Leninism is so universal in its application that any developed cadre Communist must be able, with a little briefing, to guide a union or organize sabotage—or, after the conquest of power, to guide production—in the textile industry, the taxi business, the steel industry, or the merchant marine; to criticize, with equal facility and validity, poets, biologists, movie stars, legislative representatives, and sanitary engineers; to cooperate with or destroy the character of—depending upon the line of the period—liberals, socialists, conservatives, syndicalists, and fascists, Park Avenue and Berkeley Square social lights, West Virginian and Pas de Calais proletarian leaders, the religious and the anti-religious, Western and Eastern, infidel and Turk.[17]

In his methods of work he must be able to master the widest "revolutionary experience . . . a variety and rapidity of shifting forms in the movement—legal and illegal, peaceful and stormy, open and underground, embracing small circles and large masses, parliamentary and terrorist . . . a multiplicity of forms, shades and methods of struggle, embracing all classes of modern society." [18]

Within the limits of the "general line," in just proportion to his authority, he must stand, omniscient and relentlessly certain, as the representative of the Party and the hierophant of History.

A point remains which is always included as a criterion of the Communist. Stalin and Dmitrov stress it, but observation of the most powerful of those who constitute the cadre would seem to belie it. Dmitrov places it as one of his criteria: "The closest possible contact with the masses." [19] And Stalin makes great play with the Greek myth of Antaeus on this score:

> I think that the Bolsheviks remind us of the hero of Greek mythology, Antaeus. They, like Antaeus, are strong because they maintain connection with their mother, the masses, who gave birth to them, suckled them and reared them. And as long as they maintain connection with their mother, with the people, they have every chance of remaining invincible.[20]

In actual fact, most of those who constitute the cadre have very little contact with the masses, although indirectly their work constantly involves manipulation of the masses. There is, however, something essential to the Communist reflected in this demand for "contact with the masses." "The masses" are the raw material of the social engineer. The continuing stress on "contact with the masses," when the decisive Communist cadreman has in most cases ceased to have any actual contact with the masses, is in its operative effect but a metaphorical expression of the necessity of maintaining "unity of theory and practice."

The Communist movement is not a sect. However concerned it is with preserving the purity of its doctrine, however virulent against deviators therefrom, the reason is not love of abstract truth. The true line must be defended against any deviation simply because it and it alone can be the instrument for transforming the world through control of the masses. Therefore, the Communist must never forget for a moment that the being and meaning of his unique understanding of reality will evaporate if it is hidden under a bushel,[21] if it is regarded in any other way than as a weapon with which to strike in the cause of History's future.

CYNICISM AND IDEALISM

The high tension at which the contradictions of the Communist personality type are held in quivering suspension would be intolerable were it not for another quality universally characteristic of the highest initiates, of the "wise men." Of that quality nothing is written in the books and nothing is said directly.

As the mould presses down on the human being, there are inevitable crises, each one of which has within it the potentialities of failure in the process of conditioning. It is only as a result of such a crisis, as a matter of fact, that any cadre Communist ever breaks with Communism.[22] But the weathering of such crises, the maturing of the personality towards the model of the ideal Communist, leaves its mark too. The mark it leaves is the quality which is the coping-stone of the Communist personality. It is hard to find a word to describe it adequately. When I was a Communist, I would have called it "wisdom," but it has little in common, except a certain external bearing of the man, with that tranquil and relaxed acceptance and inner peace which wisdom connotes. What it is, I think, is a pervading cynicism towards everything but the one original source of meaning of the Communist's life—faith in History and in its avatar, the Party. Not that the Party as an actuality is exempted from the cynicism. Far from it: the Party is full of corruption, inanities, unnecessary brutalities. Towards these conditions he is as cynical as towards everything else. But the Party is the Material Force (and for the Communist there exists nothing but matter in motion), the chosen vessel of History, which embodies the meaning of life.

This contradictory combination of cynicism and idealism makes possible all the other contradictions demanded of the Communist. It is the reason why fine and devoted human beings can become conscious agents of organized evil; can with equal vigor and selflessness organize a movement of Asian coolies under circumstances of incredible terror and deprivation, or direct a system of slave camps which systematically dehumanizes and destroys millions upon millions of helpless people.

Who fights for Communism must be able to fight and not to fight, to say the truth and not to say the truth, to render and to deny service, to keep a promise and to break a promise, to go into danger and to avoid danger, to be known and to be unknown. Who fights for Communism has of all the virtues only one: that he fights for Communism [23]

—so writes Bertolt Brecht, the only poet of stature Western Communism has produced.

Truly, "it is not given to all to be members of such a Party"! The inner contradictions of a self-reconstruction, which requires the suppression or destruction of most of the best instincts and attitudes of the human being and demands complete subordination of individuality, threaten at every moment to shatter the acquired personality structure into a thousand bits. Only constant exercise of the will holds it together. No wonder, then, Dmitrov's summary:

Our leading cadres should combine the knowledge of *what* they must do—with *Bolshevik stamina, revolutionary strength of character and the will power to carry it through.*[24] (Emphasis in original.)

While knowledge of what to do, Marxist-Leninist understanding, is placed first, the three concluding desiderata all have to do with the will.[25] Once let that will falter for a single moment and the human being emerges, in revolt against the elaborate structure of untruth and evil which has dominated him. There are but two possible outcomes of the conflict between the individual and the moulding process: either failure of the will to enforce dehumanization, followed by revolt and break from the Party; or the triumph of the will, fortified by cynicism and residual faith—the successful moulding of a Communist.

THREE · THE MECHANISM OF PRESSURE: THE PARTY

In the Communist view, every theory must carry with it a program of action. Therefore, as the Communist Parties have developed the Leninist theory of "the organization of professional revolutionaries," together with its corollary, the ideal image of the Communist, so they have necessarily created a system of training to carry that theory into action, to mould men in that image.

This system goes far beyond what is generally understood by training or education. It is co-extensive with the total activity of the Party. Affecting not the neophyte alone, but the Party member at every stage of his career, its pressure increases rather than decreases with development and advancement.

The responsibility for training, for the development of cadres, rests squarely upon the leading committees at every level. Specific educational commissions, schools commissions, personnel commissions exist, but it is emphasized again and again throughout Party literature that these commissions exist only as auxiliaries, that from unit bureau to Political Bureau and beyond

to the international bodies, the leading committees must themselves direct and supervise the "training of forces," not only
generally but in detail and most intimately.[1]

Of the forms at their disposal for carrying out this responsibility,
we may distinguish three broad categories: the Party system of
education proper, training in activity, and training in the daily
life of the Communist.

The system of education proper includes a ramified network
of classes of all kinds at different levels; the utilization of open
Party-controlled institutions, such as Workers Schools and
schools like the Jefferson School of Social Science in New
York; and full-time Party training schools for various levels of
development—section, district, and national training schools,
and the international schools in the Soviet Union.

Every Party meeting, from the unit level to the level of national and international conventions, committees, and bureaus,
is considered and treated as an occasion for "theoretical" analysis and discussion. If one picks up any report to a National Convention, to a National Committee meeting, to an international
Communist congress, and analyzes it, a very large proportion of
what purports to be a presentation and argument for policy is in
actual fact directed not towards the immediate issues at hand
but towards basic education. These reports become the foundation of innumerable classes and school sessions. They are studied
as texts, in detail and with theoretical elaboration. (Needless to
say, the reports and statements of Soviet leaders, whether deliv-
ered at Congresses of the Communist Party of the Soviet Union

or in their official governmental capacities at home or abroad, are the most important of these documents.)

But classes, schools, meetings, the analyses of reports—all the multifarious kinds of more or less formal Party education—are only the beginning of the story. In the very planning of Party activity, considerations of training are of outstanding importance for the selection of personnel, as for the choice of possible activities for a given group or area. Constant discussion of the work of individuals, reports to and judgments by higher committees on them, and personal leadership by the more experienced Communists, all contribute to the training process. With an over-all awareness of the critical importance of training, there is literally no aspect of Party activity which cannot be utilized as a mechanism of the training system.

But these means do not exhaust the resources at the disposal of the Party. Prototype of the totalitarian society, it considers every moment of life material for the process of moulding its members. A systematic process of observation, analysis, and criticism of intellectual and psychological personality traits, operating at all times, at every moment of personal as well as political life, is perhaps the most important of all the means of training. The intensity of this process varies, of course, with the level of commitment of the individual.

Unguarded expressions in ordinary conversations, sometimes on the most trivial subjects, are regarded as highly significant of "weaknesses of understanding" and can become the subject of long campaigns of "education." An injudicious word about the journalistic quality of the Party press, for example, can result in an elaborate probing of the "petty-bourgeois remnants" in the offender's mind, whether he be working-class by origin or not. Even common expressions must be carefully watched. Charges of "white chauvinism" have been raised because someone said that "things looked black"; and the last word of the harried male, "That's just like a woman," has more than once been seized upon as a pernicious sign of "male chauvinism."

At a higher level and on a more political plane, the concentration is upon the individual's spoken and written contributions to discussion of policy—his reports at leading committee meetings and conventions, and his articles in the press. Such statements are expected to be *exactly* on the line. A misplaced comma or a missing qualifying phrase can become the symptom of lack of "clarity," of a potential deviation.

For example, it had long been the accepted formula that "anyone who pretends to be for socialism but is against the dictatorship of the proletariat is an enemy of socialism. The attitude towards the dictatorship of the proletariat is the touchstone of the friends and enemies of socialism." Some time in the early thirties, an additional stage of refinement was added to this formulation: "Whoever claims to be for the dictatorship of the proletariat but is critical of the Soviet Union is in reality an enemy of the dictatorship of the proletariat and of socialism." Finally, in the late thirties, there sprang up another story on this house-that-Jack-built: "Whoever pretends to be a supporter of the Soviet Union but does not accept the leadership of the great Stalin is in reality an enemy of the Soviet Union, of the dictatorship of the proletariat, and of socialism." In a discussion, in the peroration of a speech, or in the conclusion of an article, to leave out any of these stages, particularly the last, was to open oneself to grave suspicion.

This is a rather gross example, since in such cases the danger signs are sufficiently apparent for a misstep to be easily avoidable. It gets difficult when the Party, striking blows rapidly to the right and to the left, has condemned a series of formulations as deviational. Here it is necessary to be very wary. Writing, for example, on the Negro question in the United States in the late thirties, when the official doctrine remained "self-determination for the Black Belt" but when in practice the Party line on the Negro question had become a reflection of the general People's Front line, one had to observe great care. Anything that might be considered a repudiation of the fundamental theoretical position could open one to charges of "right opportunism," which on the Negro question is the equivalent of "white chauvinism," of a "ruling-class attitude" towards the Negro people and all minorities. On the other hand, if the exactly right formulation on the immediate possibilities of "the struggle for Negro rights" was not correctly weighted, there was the danger of being attacked for totally failing to understand the line of the People's Front, and therefore as "objectively aiding the Fascists."

It must not be thought that the Communist subjectively considers what he is doing as avoiding traps or manipulating words. He regards it much more seriously—as an intellectual discipline absolutely necessary to arrive at truth. The necessity of learning to thread one's way through such dangers, therefore, contributes greatly in training the Communist cadre not merely to follow "the line of the Party" but to understand it and deeply accept it. That this results in an astonishing literary style is but an unfortunate by-product. That style, incidentally, can create traps for the uninitiated observer. Many a statement which seems from the outside to be merely a collection of clichés has, if properly understood, great significance. It may even, within the careful set of anti-tank obstacles which protect its flanks and rear, contain startling new theses.[2]

METHODOLOGY OF PARTY TRAINING

Organizational control alone could hardly effect a satisfactory coördination of all the diverse means and forms of Party training. Such a coördination is possible only because a commonly understood methodology inspires and regulates responsible Communist leaders in all their relations with the Party membership, neophyte and cadre, in activity and day-to-day life, as in schools and classes. So far as I know, the principles of this methodology have never been systematically written out. At one point, in connection with some plans I was making for the training of Party teachers in my District, I suggested to the legendary "Pop" Mindel, the head of the National Schools Commission— a member also of that shadowy and awe-inspiring body, the Central Control Commission—that something of the sort should be written. "You couldn't do it," he answered, "without committing a deviation on every other page. Let *them* [that is, the Russians] write it. Anyway, we know what we're doing." They did. The principles of this methodology cannot be found in any manual, but they exist in the practice and consciousness of the Party.

From the very nature of Communist theory, it is fundamental to the methodology of the training process that there can be no separation between training and life. This practical rule, derived from the concept of the unity of theory and practice, demands that all activity be considered as a school and all schooling as a continuation of activity. Or, as an article in *Cahiers du Communisme* put it: "Étudier pour agir, Agir en étudiant." [3]

At every Party training school the introductory lecture stresses this. The students are warned that what they are embarking upon "is not a vacation from the class struggle but a continuation of it at the highest level." In polemical discussion, the fiercest indictments of poor educational work are couched in such terms as "sterile academicism," "divorced from the concrete activities of the Party and the masses," "inability to link the principles of Marxism-Leninism with the day-to-day needs of the working class and the fighting line of the Party." A typical statement from an article on cadres in *The Communist* emphasizes that "theoretical educational work" must have "the closest connection with our daily mass work. But from the inevitable close connection of our theoretical work with revolutionary practice arise our concrete theoretical tasks [the program of formal education]. The Marxist-Leninist theory . . . requires that our tasks never be general but always concrete, prescribed by the special conditions of the liberation struggle of the proletariat." [4] This is not just insistence on the need for concrete illustration of theoretical points. Nor is it by any means a pragmatic or anti-theoretical attitude.

The most abstruse theoretical questions must be mastered if they form part of the corpus of Marxism-Leninism; but simultaneously, the entire theoretical structure has to be considered in the closest relationship to "the revolutionary struggle" and even to the immediate forms of that struggle. Thus, some of the most important turns in line have been heralded or reinforced by articles of Stalin on such questions as historiography or linguistics. Similarly, at one of the turning points in the early history of the Party, Lenin utilized a discussion of epistemology as the spearhead of a political move for the consolidation of his faction.

This attitude prevails throughout the Party. One can hear mere fledglings of six months' standing accuse each other of basic deviations in an argument about whether it is advisable to hold a street meeting on a corner where there are many passers-by, but where it might attract the attention of antagonistic elements, or on another corner two blocks away in a more respectable neighborhood. In such a debate "infantile leftism" and "right opportunism" may be the least erudite phrases thrown about.

Classes, therefore, and particularly training schools, are fraught with a tension far removed from the peaceful connotation that the idea of study usually evokes. "When the idea enters the mind of the masses it becomes a power," wrote Marx, and Communists take that statement with the utmost seriousness. A power for good if the ideas are "correct"; a power literally of evil—a bourgeois idea, a counter-revolutionary idea—if it is "incorrect." And if ideas in general are believed to have this living, weapon-like character, they have it intensified a thousand times when they directly affect "the vanguard party," the custodian of revolutionary truth, for if *it* goes wrong, the consequences are immeasurable.

The intensity of this feeling about ideas is strengthened by the Communist concept that there is only one correct line, that in the geometry of ideology the slightest deviation from that line inevitably ends in a complete reversal of direction. Therefore, if in a Party training school a student makes an error in a report on the proper relationship of Lenin's slogans:

The proletariat must carry out to the end *the democratic revolution,* and in this unite to itself the mass of the peasantry, in order to crush by force the resistance of the autocracy and to paralyze the instability of the bourgeoisie

and

The proletariat must accomplish *the socialist revolution,* and in this unite to itself the mass of the semi-proletarian elements of the population, in order to crush by force the resistance of the bourgeoisie and to paralyze the instability of the peasantry and petty bourgeoisie [5]

the director of the school and the teachers will examine his whole record in united-front activities, correlating any failures he has shown in practice to understand the problem of "the allies of the proletariat" with his theoretical "errors." He will find himself criticized (and, if he is a good Communist, self-criticized) not only for narrowness in periods when the Party line demanded broad work with the middle classes and liberal elements, but simultaneously for earlier errors of opportunism in periods of "sharp class struggle." By the time this ordeal is over, he will have grasped the principles of Communist strategy and tactics on the question of the allies of the proletariat—or he will be out of the Party.

In day-to-day activity, the process works in reverse. An "error" in work is immediately assigned to "theoretical weakness"; or a difference of opinion on even a comparatively minor organizational or technical question is debated and settled with constant appeals to high theoretical principles.

At upper cadre levels, these questions are taken the most seriously and fought through the most bitterly. During an international anti-war congress in Paris, where I was responsible for the British youth delegation, we ran into some problems of housing the British delegates. Such a detail, of course, should have been a matter for the front organization, the anti-war committee itself. But the situation was so snarled up that the only way out was to cut through the red tape and bring the complaint of the British Young Communist League—which had succeeded in bringing to the congress a large number of completely non-Party trade-union and Labour Party delegates—directly to the French Young Communist League in the person of its national Organizational Secretary. He showed an in-

furiatingly bureaucratic attitude, and the whole problem was
finally laid before the Communist International representative
responsible for the entire congress, on the grounds that the
attitude shown by the French comrade displayed a failure to
understand the then-just-developing People's Front line of the
Communist International. The particular practical problem was
quickly solved, but this was not the end of it. The criticisms
raised by the British Young Communist League were considered
by the French Party; the Organizational Secretary's defense
was regarded as displaying even more of an underestimation of
the People's Front policy than he had originally been accused
of; and his response to further criticisms opened him to the
accusation of holding a semi-Trotskyist position on the allies
of the proletariat. Six months after the imbroglio over housing,
he was expelled from the French Party.

This chain of circumstances, although dramatic, is by no
means unique. That things like this can and do happen gives
a powerful sanction to the continuous practice of ideological
dredging which accompanies criticism of daily work, and makes
that ideological dredging a powerful tool of training.

Should a district or a section fail markedly to meet its quota
for subscriptions to the *Worker,* then the responsible functionary
is guilty of "underestimation of the importance of the role of
the press" and, by implication, of a failure to grasp the significance of *Iskra* in the building of the Bolshevik Party—therefore,
a lack of grasp of Lenin's vitally important *What Is To Be Done?*
and of the very concept of the "party of a new type." Before
the storm blows over, he has learned in the most vivid way
many things about the theoretical and practical meaning of the
Party which he may previously have understood only formally.

At a lower level, the same methods are used, although the
possible consequences are usually less serious, in view of the

lack of experience of the members. Leaflets issued, actions taken in neighborhood organizations, organizational failures in the work of the branch, formulations in meetings—everything is grist to the mill. At this level, because of the character of the work, the kind of incident seized upon for training is often very humdrum.

An absurd example comes to mind. A leader of a large community branch had organized and successfully carried through a "legislative conference" involving a considerable number of the most prominent citizens of the area, at a time when such actions were being strongly urged by Party directives. Resolutions had been passed for a series of measures the Party was supporting; the delegates whose names were signed to the telegrams and letters to congressmen and senators were very satisfactory; there had been no divergent points of view put forward. It was altogether successful.

Shortly after its conclusion, a representative of the district bureau returned to commend (with certain well-chosen criticisms as well) the local Party leader responsible for it. He found her putting away the chairs in an empty hall. This was intolerable. She had shown lack of organizational understanding in her neglect to secure rank-and-file Party people—if she could not involve non-Party people—for such menial tasks. Her excuses and explanations led directly to a critique of her outlook as syndicalist, if not anarchist, showing a complete misunderstanding of the role of leadership, which in turn, carried to its logical conclusion, negated the very function of a vanguard party.

From top to bottom all life must be considered as training, an indissoluble unity of theory and action directed towards the one reason for existence of a Communist. The image of the iron filings oriented by a magnet is often used in Party teaching, with the qualification that one must imagine the filings each conscious and imbued with an understanding and a will which deliberately accept the power of the magnet as Truth.

"SCIENCE," CONTROL AND RESPONSIBILITY

Social interactions have for the Communist the scientifically predictable character of Newtonian physical interactions. A constant consideration of Communist training methodology, therefore, is the inculcation of an attitude which regards all social or human activity as scientifically understandable and therefore, from the Marxist-Leninist point of view, manipulable.

Since "science," then, implies not knowledge for the sake of knowing but knowledge for control, every Communist must perforce have a peculiarly responsible attitude—for everything. If something happens in China or in Bulgaria, in England or in Venezuela, in New York or Chicago, in his own section of the city or another section, he must immediately have an attitude towards it, and not merely an informed attitude or one of judgment. Like a fireman sleeping next to an alarm bell, all his faculties must be stimulated into action. What should be done? Is there anything in this situation which, in his organization, his trade union, his neighborhood, he can do? This is the way a Communist must learn to react at all times.[6]

The development of such a stance of responsibility and the elimination of all "unscientific" modes of apprehension are both vital to the moulding of the Communist personality. But the function of the constant emphasis upon them is not only to create in the Communist's mind an acceptance of the principles of Marxism-Leninism as a scientific view of the world and to develop a "responsible attitude." If this were all, these emphases could be considered simply as emphases in subject matter, in material taught; and, considered only in this way, their real methodological function would be obscured. That function is to create an awareness of life exclusively in terms of control, of power.

If thought and knowledge are invalid except in terms of the unity of theory and practice, and if the individual is responsible as one of the chosen to whom understanding is given, meaning and reality are drained out of all aspects of life not concerned with control. Enjoyment, the satisfaction of curiosity, meditation, intellectual achievement, art, and certainly all spiritual awareness are empty except insofar as they derive a secondary meaning, positive or negative, from the essential reality of human existence regarded as control of the universe.[7]

This subsuming of all the complexities of life under the single rubric of action directed towards control is so complete that it becomes in time an invisible and unrecognized condition of existence. Most of the other important attitudes Communists hold do not have this quality. They are consciously accepted and continuously defended. Even when some aspects of their attitudes are not recognized for what they are, at the least a complete rationalization is consciously, insistently, and aggressively held. But this attitude, the approach to the world which sees it exclusively as scientifically controllable, is simply taken for granted. That, perhaps, is why the arguments put forward by Communists about art, literature, love, the psyche, religion are so weak and unconvincing. What they are trying to say seems so obvious to them that their arguments have to be constructed. They have none of the power of arguments with which one has once convinced one's self.

The very form of the classics on which the whole Marxist-

Leninist dogma is founded conduces to the acceptance of all thought as directed to action. There probably has existed nowhere in history so widespread and powerful a doctrine without a systematic statement of its principles. Marxism-Leninism has no *Summa,* no *Institutes,* no *Discourse on Method,* no *Essay concerning Human Understanding*—not even an *Il Principe* or a *Leviathan.* All its foundation stones are occasional polemics. (*Capital* and *The Communist Manifesto* might be considered possible exceptions, but they too are full of polemics and their essential inspiration is polemical.) Even the philosophical canon —*The German Ideology,* the *Anti-Dühring, Materialism and Empirio-Criticism*—has this character. The authoritative political texts are all directed to a particular action or a particular controversy; to mention a few: *The Critique of the Gotha Program, What Is To Be Done?, Two Tactics, "Left Wing" Communism, Imperialism, State and Revolution, Foundations of Leninism, Problems of Leninism.*

Thought for thought's sake or for the sake of pure knowledge is, from the Marxist-Leninist viewpoint, not merely sterile; in the last analysis it is impossible. Such lucubrations, or, for that matter, literature and art not consciously motivated to an active end, have their meaning in the class interests which they reflect. But such existence is the existence of shadows. Virtue, full-bodied existence, resides only in the apprehension of life as action "to change the world."

PRESSURE

The primary elements of the methodology of the Communist training process, then, are these: uncompromising insistence on the scientific character of reality, combined with continuing stress on responsibility, in a milieu where life is training and training is life. But a further element is necessary to fuse the others together. Men are weak. They are the products of a "disintegrating society," which affects everyone—proletarian and intellectual as well as monopoly capitalist and petty bourgeois—with the vapors of its decay.[8] Historical Reality will tell in the end, if the phantasms of religion, individual integrity, family loyalty, patriotism, objective truth, and a thousand ties of tradition and upbringing can be destroyed. But their hold is strong; they are rooted in the past of the individual and are constantly reinforced by the influences which daily and hourly beat upon him from round about. The "superior" validity of Marxism-Leninism might well fail to make its impact under the hail of this never-ceasing fusillade. The growing Communist personality must be strengthened against it, the pressure relieved by a counter-pressure, that Communist truth may be received.[9]

Such counter-pressure, the fusing element of the process of Communist training, is organized systematically and relentlessly. In daily life and activity, as in classes and schools, it is built up steadily with the developing Communist maturity of the individual until it becomes a ponderable presence. Occasionally, particularly in moments of fatigue, it becomes almost intolerable; but in time it is felt not only as weight but also as support. When, with habit and growth, it has come to be largely self-imposed, it turns into a necessity of life.

Certainly this regime of pressure has its casualties. Apart from those whom it breaks and drives out of the Party (this is one of its functions, to discover the "weak"), it is also the direct cause of that frequent phenomenon of the movement, the "tired bolshevik." Utterly loyal, a cadreman of years of experience, often in a responsible position, all the resilience has gone out of his being. He drags along, fulfills his responsibilities with mediocrity, but the years of pressure have crushed him. It is still an outside force to him, one that he accepts, but one that he has never sufficiently made his own to overcome the feeling of relentless weight and thus be able to maintain his vitality.

Despite its negative results, however, pressure is an irreplaceable tool of training. It forces to the surface, out into the open where they can be handled, all the psychological and intellectual contents of the personality which must be remade—ideas, habits, prejudices, attitudes. Party training schools are set up as much with the aim of creating conditions favorable to such pressure as of inculcating theoretical material. The classes themselves, the study arrangements, the "extra-curricular activities," the relations of the students to each other and to the instructors are all calculated to produce conditions of strain to the breaking point. Every action, every statement in class, every personal characteristic is under constant attack, gruelingly systematized by formal weekly "criticism and self-criticism sessions." [10]

In the normal life and activity of the Party such hothouse conditions for the manufacture of pressure cannot be maintained, although something very like them is created in periods of crisis over the line of the Party or in the political history of individuals. "The fight for a line," "the struggle against a deviation," the handling of a disciplinary question, like the training schools, are nodes in a system of pressures.

Day in and day out, however, that system makes itself felt steadily, if less intensively than in crises and in the schools. Partly this is a result of the pure weight of tasks to be performed.[11] The demands of the movement are infinite, the forces and time at its disposal finite; and therefore, however noteworthy a success may be, much more always should be done. Whatever Communist propaganda and Communist leaders may say for external consumption, in internal evaluation the negative always enormously outweighs the positive. If something was well done, it could have been done better. If it was a decisive victory, let us say in some mass field, such as the freeing of a "political prisoner" or the success of a Party-led strike, then "the face of the Party was not brought forward." Or, if it was brought forward, "we did not capitalize on the favorable conditions by sufficient recruiting." Or, if the recruiting was satisfactory, "we are not integrating the new recruits in the W. and W. plant into Party life. The same old comrades are getting out the shop paper; none of the new, fresh blood has been involved; no New Members' Classes have been held; of 23 recruits, only 8 attended last week's meeting."

Thus, the very disproportion between the "demands of the situation" and the "forces of the Party," itself constituting an agency of pressure, creates its twin agency, the disproportion of blame to praise. It might be thought that such constant depreciation of effort expended would result in demoralization rather than in tempering. But the integral connection felt by Communists between the least important of Party acts and world-historical consequences makes the smallest success significant in ultimate and objective terms. Of course criticism must be expected. Who can rise to the heights that History demands? The Party is right always to demand more. But a glow of satisfaction exists, nonetheless, in a maneuver well executed, a mass campaign carried through to a climax, a solid accretion to Party membership. Such belief in the deep significance of every act cannot but reinforce the stance of responsibility and by that token increase the pressure.

Negative criticism thus intricately dances with magnification of the significance of every Party act to produce a double-sided pressure. The probing and testing described above, which plumbs the least "error" to its origins, reinforces that pressure. The philosophical outlook of Marxist-Leninist dialectics provides ideological sanction and manufactures inexhaustible material. Since all things are interrelated and interpenetrate one with another, and since a fact—meaningless, hardly real in itself—derives its meaning only from its external relations, the tracing of these relations outward from any fact is of the utmost significance. Intellectual and psychological facts do not differ in this respect from any other facts. So it is that a chance remark, an organizational mistake, the misconstruction of a shade of meaning in Lenin or Stalin, even a personal mannerism, is criticized in the way that it is—rarely for itself, almost inevitably as indicative of deep weaknesses which must be drawn to the surface and corrected.

The constant expectation of this kind of criticism (varying in detail and thoroughness depending on the circumstances, but implied even in the most casual daily organizational and political discussions) is a powerful factor in the creation of tension and pressure from the very early days of Party life. It develops its greatest strength, however, when the evolving Communist begins to apply this same method to himself, questioning his acts and attitudes for their "real meaning" and for their origins in "alien class sources." Dialectical introspection of this kind is most self-conscious and over-scrupulous at what one might call the pre-cadre and early cadre stages. As more maturity is attained, although a fundamentally self-critical attitude has become ingrained in the personality, its operation on one's self is likely to be restricted to more important matters. The probing of minor symptomatic expressions is reserved for younger members one is training.

Whether externally applied or internally generated, however, this questioning, probing, testing process maintains a pressure upon the personality which transforms the solidity of the previous intellectual outlook and psychic set into a state of flux in which it can be remoulded.

THE TRANSFORMATION OF THE TOTAL PERSONALITY

It is the total personality, not the intellectual outlook alone, which must be remoulded. Although logically the process of crushing the forms of the old personality precedes the construction of new forms, in actuality the two go hand in hand. But methodologically there is a difference between the two processes. While the attack upon the various aspects of the old personality is relatively undifferentiated, the principles of reconstruction differ somewhat, depending on whether it is the intellect, the will, or the emotions that are in question.

With the intellect, given the destruction of "false" values, theories, and ways of thinking, the problem is one of simple replacement with the "scientific," "objective" outlook of Marxism-Leninism.

With the will, the task is somewhat different. The will must remain fundamentally the same. Its quality, its timbre, must re-emerge from the process of bolshevization not only unflawed but strengthened. A bolshevik with a weak will is unthinkable. But the functioning of the will must be redirected; and this redirection is closely correlated with changes in the role of the faculty of judgment. The Marxist-Leninist puts the faculty of judgment on all questions but operational ones into blinkers. It functions; it considers and judges; but it does so within the limits of one primordial judgment, that the leadership of the movement is *by its nature* right. When that leadership has not spoken, judgment operates more or less independently; but once the line is laid down, it operates to confirm that line. The will must be trained to become the agent of this kind of judgment.[12]

Its power is not destroyed; rather, it is deprived of flexibility and harnessed to one great calculation of the intellect, one grand decision of judgment, which places it in the service of the Party, autonomous enough to remain strong and vibrant but contemptuous of exerting itself in individual situations. These it regards as subject to an instrumental calculus, the specific problems of which are to be worked out by a collective intelligence, in which the individual participates at his own level and in his assigned function.

The emotions present something of a problem. Somehow, however you twist and turn, they do not fit properly into the dialectical world picture. In theoretical discussions they are largely ignored. In practice a highly pragmatic attitude prevails. Where, by their very nature, they interfere with Communist effectiveness and cannot be redirected, they are suppressed. Physical fear, for example, which immobilizes, cannot be tolerated, nor can attachment to another person—filial devotion, love, or friendship—deep enough to create values independent of the Party.

Most emotions, however, are susceptible of being channeled into directions of value to the Party, and such sublimation strengthens the personality, where rigid suppression might tend to weaken it. Much of the strength of the Communist will comes from channelized emotions. Shame, for example, which for a bolshevik cannot exist in connection with his subordination to the decisions and discipline of the Party,[13] becomes a strengthening element in holding him to the line of duty. To fail in his obligations to the Party before danger or difficulty brings that emotion into play exactly as it does in the case of a well-trained soldier.

Finally, there are those emotions and passions which, unless they are developed to extremes, have neither negative nor positive value to the Party. These are regarded with neutrality. The most obvious example is sex, on which, despite occasional remarks in the literature, the Party has in practice no position and to which the training process pays no attention, except in cases where abnormality or obsession occurs. In such cases it is treated exactly like those emotions which by their very nature are interferences and is rigidly suppressed.

But whether emotions are suppressed, redirected, or ignored, they continue to provide the most difficult problems for Party training. Never fitting properly into the ideological framework, as the intellect and the will can be made to do, they are in practice constantly emerging at the most unexpected times. They create that category of difficulties which Communist organizers call, with the deepest of disgust and annoyance, "personal problems." "He has personal problems" is the nearest Communists ever come to admitting that perhaps there are some fortresses bolsheviks cannot conquer.

Nevertheless, it is to the transformation of the *whole* personality, with intellect inspiring and directing will, and will controlling the emotions, that Communist training is directed. A bitter and dramatic struggle which took place in the upper levels of the educational apparatus of the American Party in the early forties centered around this doctrine; and the outcome of that struggle conclusively vindicated it. "Pop" Mindel, the head of the National Schools Commission, had built the system of training schools of the American Party, raised a whole generation of Party teachers, and personally taught a considerable section of the leadership of the American Party. Taking his model from the Soviet Union and the international movement, he had developed—if tyrannically and with consid-

erable personal eccentricity—techniques to implement the transforming of the whole personality. He was attacked by a group
of leading members of the Educational Commission and the
Schools Commission, who formally charged him with distortions
of, and deviations from, the correct line of Marxist-Leninist
training, all summed up as "psychologizing." The Political Bureau sharply repudiated the criticisms and unconditionally en-
dorsed Mindel's teaching.

What was vindicated in the vindication of the "Mindel
method" were not the particular techniques he personally used
and taught others to use. Some of these techniques might even
have been successfully attacked had his critics attacked them
in such a way as to avoid calling into question the very essentials
of Communist training. Their criticism, however, by implication
challenged the utilization of pressure and probing, the mainstays
of "criticism and self-criticism." Without these techniques Communist personality re-formation would be impossible. Functioning in a situation where life is exhaustively conceived of as
scientific control by men responsible to History and to the
Party, they are the foundations of the methodology of Communist training.

FOUR · PHILOSOPHICAL PRESSURE: MARXISM-LENINISM

A consciously held system of ideas plays a much greater part in the dynamics of the Communist personality than of the contemporary Western personality in general. While the deepening of our understanding of the psychological springs of action in human nature is of great value, emphasis on unconscious motivation as primary can at best be fruitful in areas and periods where no strong ideational system prevails—as in the West of the past few decades, particularly in the urban centers and among the "enlightened" middle classes. The Communist, however, exists in an entirely different atmosphere. The assignment of a secondary role to his consciously held theoretical outlook can lead to serious misunderstanding of the Communist personality as well as to disastrous misjudgment of the power of Communism.[1]

In microcosm as in macrocosm, in the individual Communist as in the Communist movement, the homogeneous body of Marxist-Leninist doctrine gives shape and cohesion to the structure, operating on every level from the most abstruse to the most practical. Sufficiently flexible to enable the leadership to find a rationalization for every expediency, it nevertheless compels them to fit each new development in action or in theory into the accepted theoretical corpus. This very necessity, which is dictated by the bent and training of their own thinking, limits the degree to which expediency or pure personal-power motivations guide even the very top international leadership.[2]

At every stage of the development of the movement, every new idea, every departure from previous practice, no matter how sharp, has been presented as the unfolding of potentialities present in the theory from the beginning.[3] Lenin launched the doctrines which are the peculiar hallmark of Communism with a strict insistence that he was simply working out the original implications of Marxism, which had been debased by the Social Democrats of the late 19th century. Likewise, Stalin and his opponents in the titanic struggle of 1923-1929 propounded their ideas within the context of Marxism-Leninism; indeed, the validity of the respective positions in terms of Marxism-Leninism was made the issue in that struggle.

It is true that, since the period of the Great Purge and the launching of the Popular Front, the content of inner discussion has been largely concealed from public view, but the conclusion of that top discussion—the published basic documents of the movement—bear indelibly the marks of the Marxist-Leninist method. Stalin's Report to the 18th Party Congress of the Communist Party of the Soviet Union in 1938, Malenkov's to the 19th in 1952, and Khrushchev's to the 20th in 1956 are formed in the mode of thought of Marxism-Leninism as surely as are similar statements of the twenties. All that is different is a certain semantic camouflage—the utilization, for example, of words like "peace," "peace-loving states," "aggressor"—and the omission of the dialetical considerations which have led to the conclusions. The one must be translated, the other supplied, by the reader if the meaning and intent of these documents is to be grasped. Without this labor, he will come to the conclusion, along with the pundits and the journalists of the thirties or the fifties, that "Stalin has given up the idea of the world expansion of Communism and is concentrating on Russia," or that "Khrushchev is a typical administrator and business man, whose Marxism is only a ritualistic remnant." [4]

From the international leadership down through the entire cadre, the Communist cannot be understood without a knowledge of the theoretical doctrines he holds. The explicitness of consciousness, the precision of understanding, differ from level to level. As it is conditioned at the top by possession of power and the peculiar national circumstances in which that power is exercised, so it is often conditioned at the bottom by other factors.

Undoubtedly there are many Communists in comparatively important positions who would find it impossible to carry on even a relatively simple Marxist-Leninist theoretical discussion on philosophical or economic questions. Undoubtedly many of them see themselves as "practical men" and even look with considerable scepticism on the emphasis the movement constantly puts on theory. But the least "theoretical" among them looks at the world through the same categories and acts in it with the same methodology as the most "theoretically developed" Communist. His understanding of the attitudes he holds may be shallow. To him they may seem to be simply common sense, to the casual observer but a set of prejudices; yet analysis will show that they are far from a random collection of common-sense beliefs and prejudices. They have the special quality of being logically and mutually interrelated—over-simplifications, perhaps, but, still, reflections of the complex intellectual system

of Marxism-Leninism. The Communist ¬tenographer who un-
hesitatingly steals confidential papers from the files of her em-
ployer may not be versed in Marxist-Leninist moral theory, but
her moral principles are firmly based upon it. The trade-union
organizer who pulls a suicidal strike for political reasons may
never have studied *What Is To Be Done?* or be able to carry
on polemics against "spontaneity" or "economism," but Lenin's
principle of the "subordination of trade-union consciousness to
political consciousness" determines his everyday activity.

For the Communist, life takes place in terms of the categories
of Marxism-Leninism as surely as the normal eye sees in terms
of color or the monochromatic in lights and shades. For the
fully developed, well-trained Communist, there is no conceivable
area of life, of action, even of speculation, in which the judi-
cious use of Marxist-Leninist theory cannot quickly yield certainties and clarities which fit with precision into the well-
ordered pattern of his total outlook.[5] That is why the Communist
leader will not hesitate to tell a physicist that the principle of in-
determinancy represents unclear thinking and imperfect science,
or to instruct the novelist in the principles of his craft. It is also
why the physicist or the novelist, if he is a good Communist, will
take these judgments more seriously than he would those of
leaders in his own profession.

A CLOSED MATERIAL UNIVERSE

The accepted universality of Marxism-Leninism and the ordered
rationality of existence which for the Communist results therefrom make his world a sure, well-mapped place, as much a
contrast to the world of the non-Communist Western mid-

century mind as are the ordered gardens of England to the spaces of a virgin continent.

But a universe to be mappable must be finite, limited. This is indeed the first characteristic of the Marxist-Leninist universe. Despite its formal claims to unlimitedness and freedom, dialectical materialism is the philosophy of a closed universe. "Its infinity," someone has said, "is a tame infinity." There is nothing unknowable, only "that which is not yet known." What is not knowable in Marxist-Leninist categories, what cannot be transformed through theory materialized in practice from "the thing in itself" to "the thing for us" simply does not exist—or, more exactly, exists only as a mental phantasm, a socially produced distortion of the real. For "all that is real is rational"; and the truly rational is subject to the confirmation of practice. For the Communist, what he cannot act upon is neither rational nor real.[6]

I well remember the great sureness which I felt when I began to accept Marxism-Leninism. It was not a feeling of dogmatic certainty, in the sense that I felt I knew the answers to every possible question or that I had accepted an authority which could give them to me. Rather, it was the vision of the correlation of all aspects of experience, each with each, the certainty that an answer could be found to every meaningful question and that everything which did not fit could be dismissed as meaningless, unreal. Whole realms could be dismissed as unsubstantial vaporings without weakening the architecture of one's view of life. That this was achieved through denying the existence of the richest areas of human experience, the ideal and the spiritual, seemed unimportant at the time in comparison with the lifting of doubt and anxiety that accompanied it. Certainly the specific and rather intellectual form that this took in my case is not typical; but the essential content of it has been expressed to me by dozens of Communists of widely varying levels of intellectual background.

Universally, the loss of this security which arises from the possession of a limited and known universe presents a major problem to those who break with the Party. Even for the least intellectually interested, this is not simply a question of friends, associates, habits; it is the loss of a way of thinking which makes it comparatively easy to find answers to everything: the simple moral problems of everyday life; how to vote in a trade-union meeting; what to think about the latest newspaper headline. Life for the Communist contains no mystery, and the fight back to the acceptance of the glorious human fate of living with mystery is difficult indeed.

LIFE AND THOUGHT AS CONTROL:
THE UNITY OF THEORY AND PRACTICE

The Marxist-Leninist universe is not only a limited and knowable universe; it is a controllable universe. There is no valid mode of knowing but "science"—not science understood as the knowledge of regularities in phenomena; but science regarded, within the limits it has reached at any time, as absolute truth (the Hegelian "relative absolute"). Such knowledge gives power. What does not give power, what is not "confirmed by practice," is false. "If what our practice confirms is the sole, ultimate and objective truth, then from this must follow the recognition that the only path to this truth is the path of science, which holds the materialist point of view." [7] "The question whether objective truth is an attribute of human thought—is not a theoretical but a *practical* question. Man must prove the truth, i.e., the reality and power, the 'this-sidedness' of his thinking in practice." [8]

The denial of significance to non-material and non-scientific categories is characteristic not only of Marxist-Leninists but also of other materialists and positivists of many varieties. The thorough-going intensity, however, with which the Communist absorbs these beliefs and lives by them, in a way that is very rare in the modern world, distinguishes him from these others. And this seems to be integrally connected with the concept of thought and life as control. Pragmatists and instrumentalists, it is true, also tend to reduce the content of thought to its practical and instrumental effects; but the role of control, of practice, in Marxist-Leninist theory is both greater and less than in pragmatism-instrumentalism. More, because control over existence is not simply a goal of thought but its essential being; less, because theory is not reducible to practice, but indissolubly united with it in a relationship where neither exists without the other, where each determines the other, permitting independent validity neither to abstract theory nor to empirical practice. It is a strange marriage of rationalism and empiricism, this unity of theory and practice which forms the intellectual mode of existence of the Communist.[9]

A great deal more could be said about the philosophical foundations of Marxism-Leninism, but that is beyond the scope of this book. On the philosophical level, as on the ethical, the social, the economic, and the political, all that can be done is to indicate those aspects of Communist theory which are central and which form the intellectual mould of the Communist personality. These are the nodes around which Communist teaching, formal and informal, is organized. Unfortunately for the student who has not had the dubious privilege of undergoing

Communist training, the Marxist-Leninist literature itself, in its copiousness, gives little guide to these nodal points so well understood by Communist leaders and teachers. All that can be done here is to give some indications which may help to enrich the reader's comprehension.

MORAL THEORY

It has already been shown in passing how the moral theory of Marxism-Leninism operates in practice to identify the good with the interests of the revolution, which are in turn identical with the decisions of the Party. Lenin states it quite clearly: "We repudiate all morality that is taken outside of human, class concepts. . . . We say that our morality is entirely subordinated to the interests of the class struggle of the proletariat. Our morality is deduced from the class struggle of the proletariat . . . is subordinated to the interests of the class struggle of the proletariat. . . . When people talk to us about morality we say: For the Communist, morality consists entirely of compact united discipline and conscious mass struggle against the exploiters." [10]

This is one of the few statements in the classic literature on Communist ethics; but the oral tradition, which is more copious, is equally clear and distinct. Moral ideas have no independent status. "Good," "right," "justice" have meaning only in relation to a specific social situation; and in class society that social situation is the class struggle. Therefore there is not and cannot be any over-all system of morality; there is only class morality. When some young comrade, raising an objection to a piece of deception or arguing in a class about moral questions, uses the words "right" or "good," the inevitable, the standard answer is: " 'Right? Good?' as Lenin used to say, *'for what class?'* "

For the individual Communist, moral questions are thus reduced to a calculus: "Will this act help or hurt the revolution—the Party?" [11] It is a calculus in which he has the aid of the pronouncements of the Party on many questions; but even in the minor ones where he does not have this assistance, he is spared all the difficulties that attend the attempt to live a moral life. Again the principle of limitation. The dark responsibility of those who, by conscious thought or through childhood training, feel at least dimly in every act of significance their freedom to do right or wrong is not the Communist's.

Freedom, like right, good, and justice, has no independent being. It is but "the recognition of necessity." With the knowledge Marxism-Leninism gives of the character of necessity, all that the Communist has to do to make a "moral" choice is to exercise his intellectual judgment. "Freedom of the will . . . means nothing but the capacity to make decisions with real knowledge of the subject. Therefore the *freer* a man's judgment is in relation to a definite question, with so much the greater *necessity* is the content of this judgment determined; while the uncertainty, founded on ignorance, which seems to make an arbitrary choice among many different and conflicting possible decisions, shows by this precisely that it is not free, that it is controlled by the very object it should itself control. Freedom therefore consists in the control over ourselves and over external nature. . . ." [12]

Freedom is control. Right action is also control, for it is action based on knowledge of necessity. If it is action which goes against necessity, then in the long run it is bound to fail to control. It is wrong, evil, immoral. It would be a mistake to conclude from this, however, that the Communist position is simply the pragmatic one that the good is what succeeds, that right is might. Just as Marxist dialectics insists that it is necessary to grasp simultaneously the concepts "all that is rational is real" and "all that is real is rational" if the true unity of the theoretical and practical aspects of existence is to be achieved—so also in the moral sphere. "Right is might" must be integrally conceived with "might is right." The individual Communist believes that what he does for the proletarian revolution is right because the proletarian revolution is fated to be victorious; and that it will be victorious because what is done to bring it about is right. There is no dilemma, therefore, between the "inevitability of socialism" and the duty to act to bring it about.

HISTORICAL MATERIALISM

"Freedom is the recognition of necessity," and Necessity operating in society is called History. As the natural sciences interpreted in the dialectical manner make up the positive content of dialectical materialism, exhibiting the laws of necessity in nature, so historical materialism makes up its content and exhibits its laws in society.

For the historical materialist, "there are no accidents." [13] In human society, in economic development, in political struggle, the dialectical laws of history act with all the inexorability of the laws of nature. The only difference is the form of the dialectical interplay. In society one of the elements is human consciousness. The elaborate "superstructure" created through it—legal, political, religious, aesthetic, and philosophical—reflects the way in which consciousness is determined by the material conditions of its existence and in reflex action in turn affects these conditions. Interpretation of any individual situation, therefore, must take into account the action of consciousness and its constructs.

But this is not fundamental. Although consciousness and its ideological superstructure play their part, and a necessary part, in the working out of history, history is determined in its essence by the material conditions of men's existence—the way in which they produce. "The mode of production in material life determines the general character of the social, political and spiritual processes of life. It is not the consciousness of men that determines their existence, but, on the contrary, their social existence determines their consciousness." [14]

Therefore, the real causes of social phenomena are not to be found in consciousness or in the ideological "superstructure"— not in ideas, or ideals, or the conscious intentions of men. In whatever ideological guise men may act out the drama of history, for whatever reasons they may think they act, they are impelled by the laws of development of "the material mode of production." They may be completely unconscious of these causes, or dimly conscious, or—with the coming of the proletariat on the stage of history—they may, as Marxists, understand them. In this last case, and this last case only, are they truly free, because they recognize the necessity which moves them and they accept it. It is this recognition and acceptance (only possible, it is true, once society has reached the stage of the emergence of the pro-letariat, and easier for the proletarian than for others to reach), not the physical fact of being a proletarian, which gives free-dom and power.

So it is that whatever may happen—defeat or victory or long-continued tension—in small events or in large, the Communist is possessed of a confidence in ultimate victory which permeates his whole being. The arrogance sometimes displayed by Com-munists in discussions with others and by the Soviet leaders in their international pronouncements is not the result of funda-mental lack of self-confidence, which some claim; it is bad-mannered impatience with backward persons who don't seem to understand the most obvious truths. "As is well known, stones are good to eat."

Defeats and setbacks may be due to unavoidable circumstances of the ebb and flow of development, or they may be due to imperfect understanding of the laws of history—"lack of clarity"—but they never impinge on the certainty that these laws are, in general, understood and, being understood, make the Communist invincible.

That invincibility seems to him of the same order of certainty as the daily rising of the sun—based on the same kind of understanding of the underlying laws that govern visible phenomena. Are not changes in "the mode of production" the moving forces of history? Can "the mode of production" long remain unchanged if there is disharmony between its two components, if the "relations of production" (the forms of human social organization) are inadequate to the demands of new and powerful "forces of production" (the means of production and the technological level of men)? Will not antiquated relations of production, systems of organization based on obsolete productive forces, certainly be "burst asunder" by the power of new and progressive forces of production?

It has happened before to slave society, to feudal society, and it is happening before his eyes to capitalist society. Capitalist relations of production are fetters upon the modern forces of production. These fetters must be thrown off. And this can only come about through the action of men associated with the new forces of production, the proletariat, in struggle against other men associated with the old relations of production, the capitalist class. As it is put in Communist schools: "The Ford plant will not rise and march on Wall Street, but the Ford workers will rise against the men of Wall Street. And, whatever their motivations, in whatever political forms the struggle occurs, however justified their grievances and violent their indignations, the fundamental forces moving them and the guarantee of their victory arise from the power of the new forces of production."

The class struggle and the messianic role of the proletariat are but reflections of "the material transformation of the economic conditions of production which can be determined with the precision of natural science. . . ." [15] He who stands with the proletariat, who accepts the class struggle as the dominating form of history, places himself on the side of the forces whose triumph can be determined "with the precision of natural science."

THEORY OF THE PARTY

It would seem that the certain power of the forces of production would deny any role to conscious planned activity. Moving glacier-like in their appointed way until their mighty force, expressed by the proletariat, sets off the avalanche of social revolution, they would scarcely appear to depend at all on consciousness. But although the material productive forces, expressing themselves in the modern instance through the action of the proletariat, are the decisive forces of history, the very certainty of this "natural" process demands, by a turn of Marxist dialectics, the most conscious of conscious human activity—the activity of the Communist Party.

The necessity of the underlying forces can only be expressed through men—and men as they are, that is, men who act through their consciousness. Consciousness of injury, of oppression, of immediate ways of resisting that oppression, however, is not enough. Yet this sort of consciousness, "trade-union consciousness," is all that the spontaneous development of the class struggle will generate in the mind of the proletariat. Marxist revolutionary consciousness, socialist consciousness "can arise only on the basis of profound scientific knowledge. . . . The vehicles of science are not the proletariat, but the *bourgeois intelligentsia*. . . . Thus, socialist consciousness is something introduced into the proletarian class struggle from without . . . and not something that arose within it spontaneously. . . ." [16] While economic conditions bring into existence the proletariat as a force which can revolutionize society, it is only the understanding of those conditions and of that possibility which can make the possibility actuality. "Without a revolutionary theory there can be no revolutionary movement." [17]

But how are the two prerequisites—a potentially revolutionary class without revolutionary consciousness and the revolutionary theory in the minds of "bourgeois intellectuals" like Marx and Lenin—to be linked, to be fused, into the necessary unity of theory and practice? That linkage, that fusion, can only be brought about by an organization of men who understand revolutionary theory, men who, by that understanding, gain material force from the proletariat, and lead the proletariat to the seizure of power. ". . . the victory of the proletarian revolution, the victory of the dictatorship of the proletariat, is impossible without a revolutionary party of the proletariat . . . a party of the new type, a Marxist-Leninist party, a party of social revolution, a party capable of preparing the proletariat for decisive battles against the bourgeoisie and of organizing the victory of the proletariat revolution. . . ." [18]

A materialist sacrament, the visible sign of things invisible, the Party concentrates all the Communist's devotion. The concept of the Party is the unifying concept in his mind. Through it the metaphysical, the moral, and the social aspects of his thought are focussed upon his activity. It is the indispensable meeting place where thought, belief, and emotion are unified with action; and it is the living repository of that Necessity and History which vindicate the meaning and certainty of his existence.

With the concept of the Party we complete the survey of the general concepts of the ideology of the Communist. Derived from these, however, are a set of operational concepts and analyses which guide the Party's action and mediate theory to practice. For convenience, they can be subdivided into two groupings. The first has to do with the arena of activity, with analyses of society subordinate to and derived from the basic theories of historical materialism—outstandingly, the central dogmas of economics and politics: the theory of value, with its derivatives, and the theory of the state with the associated theory of the dictatorship of the proletariat. The second, Marxist-Leninist strategy and tactics, is operational in a stricter sense, derived from the concept of the Party and directly linked with action.

ECONOMIC THEORY

The complex of ideas—value, surplus value, exploitation, capitalist crisis—which since Marx's day has been so powerful an element in the socialist mind, is brought to an apocalyptic point in the Communist outlook. The function of political economy in the Communist world-view is far removed from that of economic science as usually understood today. Its function is much more that of a cosmological birth-and-death myth. It does not explain the movement of prices on the market or any such hum drum phenomena. Instead, it pretends to exhibit the unfolding of the inner characteristics of commodity production, which bring capitalism to birth, develop its power, and condemn it to death. Here the general movement of the forces of History, which govern all human existence and all societies, is manifested for this society, for capitalism. Armed with this myth, the Communist "understands" not only how capitalism is formally doomed by History because of the "contradictions between its productive forces and its relations of production," but how materially, innately, it is fated to die by the very character of its particular existence.

A few simple elements express this vision and are so deeply indoctrinated by Communist teaching that (even if the complexities of the theory are not remembered) they remain fundamental to the consciousness of every developed Communist:

The value of commodities represents the socially necessary labor incorporated in them. In capitalist production, labor itself is a commodity and receives only what is necessary to maintain and reproduce it. The difference between the value the workers add to the social product and the value they receive is surplus value, the social toll extracted by the capitalist class. This exploitation is the central social feature of capitalism. It is not the result of the character of members of the class, it is implicit in the system.

Exploitation is integral to capitalism. But this would be no reason why capitalism should not continue to exist indefinitely. Injustice of itself does not doom a society; only material force can change the world. From exploitation, however, arises dialectically the certain fate of capitalism, the capitalist crisis.

Marx's reasoning and analysis in deriving his theory of crisis from the theories of value and surplus value are not unsubtle nor without ingenuity. But in the Communist *mythos,* the detailed arguments are forgotten; the picture is stark and clear. The capitalists absorb a greater and greater share of the results of production. As the "absolute and relative impoverishment" of the working class deepens, the market for the products of capitalist industry begins to disappear. The forces of production have created a plethora of goods; the capitalists cease to find it profitable to produce; the masses starve; they are impelled into action; revolution. However primitive this argument, it has an impelling simplicity. Here we are not dealing with academic theories of over-production or under-consumption; this is an apocalyptic prophecy, a prophecy of doom for the enemy and victory for the elect.

With the contributions of Lenin and Stalin, the apocalypse is dated, brought close. The Leninist theory of imperialism presents this crisis expanded on an international scale. The development of massive monopolies, product of the union of finance and industrial capital, locked in titanic struggles for the undeveloped portions of the world, rises to a climax in internecine imperialist wars between the great capitalist powers. The colonial peoples challenge the capitalists. Then comes the proletariat's opportunity to overthrow the whole system.

The Soviet revolution, removing a large section of the world from the capitalist system, creates the final tension. Stalin's theory of the "general crisis" sets forth the conditions of this last exacerbation of the contradictions of capitalism and places the end of the world-wide system on the order of the day.

It matters little that the economic developments of the hundred years since Marx contradict his theories at every point. The political realities of the era seem to the Communist to confirm them. Although the victories of Communism arise from the power of the Red Army, from the corroding infiltration of conspiratorial Communist Parties, and from the weak and divided counsels of the West, every such advance strengthens in the Communist mind the certainty of the conquering correctness of his theory. In this field, as in all others, it would be a mistake to underrate the power of Communist theory in the Communist personality because it is rationally or empirically refutable. Communist theory is powerful not because it is true; most obviously it is not. It is powerful because *it is believed*. Each aspect may be intellectually weak enough on its own, but in the total theoretical structure each strengthens the other and a unified view is created. Theories which, standing on their own, would be ludicrous take on the seeming luminosity of truth.

THEORY OF THE STATE

As with economic theory, so it is with political theory. Tested by the actual development of state forms—particularly over the past half-century—the Marxist-Leninist theory of the state is patently untenable. But its truth for the Communist is its congruence with the rest of the theoretical structure. Rather than the facts confuting the theory, the theory transforms the facts. If at first sight it does not seem that, for example, Harry Truman was the picked representative of a ruthless concentrated capitalist class, "the head of a band of militant imperialists," as the *Daily Worker* once called him, then something is wrong with first sight. A further examination of the facts is necessary to arrive at their "true inner significance."

The state is part of the superstructure. However complex its forms, and the moral, political, and juridical ideas which justify those forms, its character is determined by the substructure, by the existing relations of production. Its function is to defend by force the position of the ruling class and to maintain by force the oppression and exploitation of the ruled. Everything else the state may do or seem to do is accidental to its essence and to be ignored in serious political analysis.

Since it is an instrument of pure force, functioning to preserve existing relations of production, progress can come about only through the application of force to it, that is, through its violent overthrow. This doctrine is true of every society except the Socialist society. Only the proletarian state, though itself a dictatorship, as all states must be, will in the end "wither away." It will not have to be violently overthrown because the proletariat can, by doctrine, never stand in the way of the developing forces of production. Oppressing no one but the exploiters of the past, it will, when it has destroyed them, no longer need a state apparatus.

There are times, of course, when a current Party line, such as the People's Front position of the thirties, seems to be based upon an analysis which would contradict the dogmatic certainty of the theory of the state. Where such a line is sufficiently long-lasting and thoroughly carried out so that the explanation of "tactical maneuver" is not fully satisfactory, the basic purity of the doctrine is protected by adroit gymnastics based on some casual remark of Marx's or Lenin's about temporary situations when the state machine can be neutralized to a degree because of a momentary balance of class forces. But then it is emphasized even more categorically that this in no way changes the essential character and function of the state.

The living result of Marxist-Leninist political theory is this: the existing capitalist state is force and the existing capitalist state is the enemy. Against it, all measures are justifiable, and the Communist must expect it to take all measures against him. Its Bill of Rights, its legal protections, are but shams, hiding the naked reality of power. Insofar as the need for camouflage creates contradictions which can be utilized for tactical purposes in the struggle, well and good. The Communist laughs cynically and works them for all that is in them.

He prides himself that, unlike the "confused" liberals and Social Democrats with their "illusions" about democracy and constitutional safeguards, he knows how things really are. This viewpoint not only enables him to adopt an absolutely free, immoral, and treasonable attitude toward his own country; it also provides him with the ability to accept, even to glorify, those horrors of the Soviet dictatorship which are pressed upon his attention so strongly that he is unable to deny them point-blank as lies and distortions. Force is the nature of states, and therefore the dictatorship of the proletariat must also be the rule of force. It is "the rule—unrestricted by law and based on force— of the proletariat over the bourgeoisie." [19] But this dictatorship is the agent of History, of the future, of the good. Force is force, violence is violence; but proletarian force is as good as the force of the capitalist state is bad.[20] Force, power, is ᵗhe law of history. The only important question is the end for which it is exerted; on which side do you stand?

Other theories of the state besides the Leninist stress the importance of the criterion of power; but for the Communist it is not an idea held abstractly or as an ultimate explanation; it is direct and personal in application. "Get out in a demonstration and get cracked on the head by a police club; you'll learn more about the state in thirty seconds than in a year of reading."

The whole complex of politics is reduced to the operational simplicity of a battle plan. Communist political activity becomes simply and directly a war for the destruction of the enemy state—a war waged on a hundred levels with indirect, subsidiary, and flanking operations that on the surface look far removed in substance or in form from the final aim, but all of which have meaning only in terms of that final aim.

STRATEGY AND TACTICS

In this war all the ramifications of Communist theory—its philosophy, its moral theory, its historical and sociological doctrine—have their outcome. Here the unity of theory and practice is attained; Marxist-Leninist theory "realizes" itself in the material world from which it arose. Communist strategy and tactics, in which the edifice of theory culminates, are at the same time the operational doctrine of action—the war doctrine of Marxism-Leninism. Its precepts are stated in terms of military science and cover the whole range of Communist activities. It gives the tone, it is the form in which the Communist attitude of control is made manifest in life.

Communist strategical doctrine deals with the analysis by the general staff, the Party, of the elements of action: of the main force (the proletariat and, in particular, the state power of "the dictatorship of the proletariat"); of the reserves of the proletariat (the colonial peoples, the peasantry, the middle classes); of the situation of the enemy and the direction of the next blow against him at any stage. The field of action is international; the duration of the struggle indefinite; and the modes of struggle as infinitely complex as society itself. The choice of these modes, of forms of struggle and forms of organization, is the task of tactics; and the decisive criterion of tactical leadership is the ability to "locate at any given moment that particular link in the chain of processes which, if grasped, will enable us to hold the whole chain and to prepare the conditions for achieving strategic success." [21] Yesterday, the exploitation of anti-fascism; today, of the nationalism of Nasser, Sukarno, Nehru, Castro.

Tactics must always be subordinated to strategy, strategy to the theoretical presuppositions of Marxism-Leninism.[22] But no other limitations, of habit or custom, lethargy or fear, no criteria external to the system, are allowed to enter into strategical and tactical thinking. The Communist attitude on the peasantry, the middle classes, national minorities, women, Negroes, Jews is determined solely by strategical and tactical considerations. Of course, most of those who enter the Communist movement do so with already existing attitudes on some of these questions, developed originally from personal thought based on many considerations. Insofar as they become real Communists, however, every attitude they hold on such issues is strictly derived from strategical and tactical considerations.

This strategical and tactical approach to problems is not limited to major questions. It permeates every attitude at every level of the Party—whether it be the decision of a leading committee or the personal act of an individual Communist. Within the general line, there is a strategy and tactics for every level. The subordinate leader, as well as the individual himself in many circumstances, is expected to work out his own tactics, and sometimes even to develop a limited strategy. Strategy and tactics is a matter for every Communist to master, not simply a question for the top leadership. In every situation he must ask himself: "What is the objective situation, what forces do we have, what allies can be won, what is the first thing to be done, what mechanisms are available or can be created?"

Whether it is actually thought out as formally as this or becomes an acquired habit of mind, this is the kind of approach which in the Communist takes the place of the moral judgment of the best moments of other men, as it takes the place of the rationalized selfishness of their worst moments. From the course to be pursued in a trade union or a P.-T.A., to the position of the Party in a Presidential election, from fraternization with Negroes to justification of the Soviet slave camps, no matter how different the problem, the criterion is always the same: what is strategically and tactically desirable?

"What is to be done?" is a continuing question, the only important question for the Communist. To do, to act, to control, is his being. His only "live option" is what to do in the specific situation. All the rest History determines. What History has determined, Marxist-Leninist theory both passively reflects and actively brings about—brings it about through Marxist-Leninist men, through conscious Communists.[23]

It is in men, Communist men, that theory and practice fuse. Thus they become History: "We are the future." Arrogating to themselves a quality, the unity of thought and action, which is manifestly absurd in men—which Western thought has always attributed as a distinguishing quality to God—they acquire a strength and confidence which, like the fearful evil they bring into being, can only be described as Luciferian.

FIVE · PSYCHOLOGICAL PRESSURE

The moulding of Communists is in large part a transformation of the psyche, a sort of psychotherapy or psychosurgery. But an apparent contradiction exists. There is a highly successful psychological practice and no apparent psychological theory of Party training—a "locked-door mystery." As usual in the locked-door mystery, however, the contradiction is more apparent than real. There is a definite set of presuppositions about the character of the human personality, derived deductively from Marxist-Leninist philosophy, which are *implicitly* held by Communists and on the basis of which Communist psychosurgical procedures are conducted. It is, one might say, an unconscious psychology, although certainly not a psychology of the unconscious.

Being entirely implicit, the principles of this Marxist-Leninist psychological theory can only be derived indirectly. Therefore I rely, on the one hand, on consideration of my own practice and the observed practice of others while I was a Communist, and, on the other hand, on the psychological implications of the metaphysical and epistemological principles of Marxism-Leninism.

To begin with, it should be stressed that the problems which have concerned men looking at man, from Augustine to Freud and Jung, simply do not exist for Marxist-Leninists. It is a natural corollary of the idea of a limited universe that human personality is considered in strictly limited terms. The idea of the unconscious is "counter-revolutionary mysticism"; it is as manifestly unreal as the idea of a soul. "Original sin" and "anxiety" alike are concepts without content or meaning—the product of "idealist" obfuscation of the true nature of man. This approach, fully consonant with and derivable from ideological sources, is confirmed, as it were, by the developed Communist's subjective experience. Fear, worry, jealousies, feelings of being underestimated—such subjective problems enter his mind and have to be dealt with in terms of Communist self-analysis. But that mode of self-awareness which the Christian, the humanist, the analyst describe respectively as the sense of original sin, the tragic sense, or "floating anxiety," is unknown to him.

The only explanation of this phenomenon I have seen seems to me untenable: that the Party, harnessing "aggression" and providing it with suitable and accepted objects, externalizes it and relieves inner tension. But the developed Communist is, on the whole, remarkably free of aggressive attitudes towards the symbols against which the Party mobilizes the masses (including its own neophyte members). Indignation, moral or otherwise, towards hostile symbols is almost entirely confined to agitational occasions, when the use of rhetoric perhaps stirs up a certain amount of fervor in the speaker himself. I am not maintaining that the indignation voiced by the Communist agitator is insincere. Certainly he thoroughly believes it and, under such circumstances, acts it. But in private conversation, in day-to-day life, the emotional attitude of the developed Communist is highly sober.[1]

In fact, if a developing Communist gives vent to such emotions he will be—reasonably gently—rebuked: "What do you expect from the class enemy?" The question is put in a matter-of-fact, conversational tone. Energy is not to be frittered away on emotionalities. Furthermore, the scientist and the military officer—and leaders of the revolution must be both—have to keep their judgment free of such involvement. The Communist must never be hastened, delayed, diverted, or provoked. All his emotional energy, it is true, must be at the service of his mission, but only indirectly, as a central powerhouse activating his total life, not fed out to this or that symbol. And no one emotion alone, but all of this powerhouse is so harnessed.

Some displacement of internal conflict obviously takes place. But, if I were to hazard a choice of concepts to explain that displacement, I would tend to think rather in terms of the approach of Jung than that of Freud or Fromm. Communism has created an ideology, reinforced by and "explaining" a set of archetypal images, which externalizes upon the material world—successfully, if demoniacally—not this or that conflict within the personality, but the entire inner human drama. Externalized, the contradictions are overcome, their fertility is destroyed, and the open dimension of man is cut off. All psychic energy is fixed upon a correlated set of ideas and images which can be apprehended in action in a limited material world. This operation stunts the person, placing him at the service of power, but it does remove the ache.

Along some such lines, I think, the explanation of the peculiar psychological anesthesia of the Communist must be sought. But, whatever the explanation, the fact remains that in Party theory the human personality is a phenomenon without mystery, without lights and shades.

THE THEORY OF PERSONALITY—A DIALECTICAL DRAMA

The conceptual framework of this theory of personality is neither empirical nor introspective in its origins; it is derived strictly deductively from philosophical principles. Here the underlying Hegelian dialectical drama survives with hardly a change except the renaming of the *dramatis personae*. The words "alienation" and "realization" are rarely used in Communist discussion, but in the more humdrum dress with which the Parties have replaced the scintillating philosophical paradoxes of Hegel and the young Marx, these concepts are the foundation of Communist psychological practice.

Marxism, claiming to be scientific, cannot deny the biological antecedents of society. But all Communist affect flows from the drama of the history of society; and in that drama, the primeval fact is parthenogenesis. Man *qua* man is neither the result of a creative act of God nor of the process of evolution. He comes into being as a result of his own act. "Men can be distinguished from animals by consciousness, by religion, by anything else you like. They themselves begin to distinguish themselves from animals as soon as they begin to *produce* their means of subsistence." [2]

In the beginning is man, self-produced, integral—materialist replica of the Absolute Idea. He produces to live, and his mode of producing is his life. At this point, although primitive and limited, man's consciousness clearly and truthfully reflects reality, as the circumstances of his existence are integral with his role as producer. But, negating itself, the very process of human pro-

duction brings about division of labor and the class division of
society. Man is split. Alienated from himself, he forgets the
pristine glory of his role as producer. He sees himself as an individual with individual interests over against society—and this
whether he is a member of the oppressed or oppressing class.
Man, like the Absolute Idea, has become estranged from himself.

Yet, as with the Absolute Idea, this alienation is a necessary
descent into the inferno of "otherness," the better in the end to
realize himself. After the varieties of class society have run their
course, and in doing so created greater possibilities of produc-
tiveness (awareness), the negation is negated. Unity is again
achieved in modern Communism, the apotheosis of primitive society, on the higher productive level created by epochs of class
society. In this new community, in this "real community the
individuals obtain their freedom in and through their association." [3] With the overcoming of class division, the split in man
is healed. No longer is he alienated from himself, no longer
does he exist in two capacities, as individual and as a member
of society.

Such a state of consciousness, in which the individual thinks
and acts in perfect unity with the community, would seem to
differ little from the presumed consciousness of an ant or a bee;
but to one possessed by the Marxist *mystique,* it takes on an
aura of freedom, external and internal, which is logically inex-
plicable. Under Communism, not only does man pass "from pre-
history into history"; he passes from congenital sickness of soul
to health.

But in class society, where alienation still prevails, the personality of man is the product of tension between the class influences shaping him and his conscious understanding. Both
arise from the operation of the mode of production; that they

are separate and opposed is but the result of the alienation in
human production itself. Yet they come into sharp conflict; and
the degree to which their tension approaches unity or opposition
depends upon the degree to which at a given time the forces of
production and the relations of production are in consonance or
conflict.

So far the underlying theory of personality. But not being explicitly stated, it is not generalized. Insofar as it is implicitly developed, it is for practical psychosurgical purposes, aɪɟ therefore it is directed to the special circumstances of the Communist.
Other men, in the past or now, may have found or may find
ideologies which more or less objectively mask the contradiction
and anesthetize the radical neurosis of alienated man. The
Communist, however, is a different kettle of fish. Living in de-
vout anticipation of the consummation of non-alienated Communist society, he partakes, in advance as it were, of its non-
neurotic simplicity of personality. At least he does insofar as he
is a Communist, insofar as he has overcome his original nature
as a product of capitalist society. The "adjusted" Communist
is he in whom the influence of class society has been eliminated
by being brought under the control of a Marxist consciousness.
All the "individualistic" traits which spoil his unique vocation as
professional revolutionary, integrally unified with the Party, have
been destroyed. The contradiction within him is overcome.

The Party being surrogate for the future society, the Communist has therefore the possibility of achieving the clarity of
vision denied to other members of a class society. But he has
not only the possibility, he has the duty to do so. In fact, achieving such a mode of being is synonymous with becoming a true
Communist.[4]

To bring this about is the essence of the Party's practice in the moulding of the personality and is the rationale behind the complex of methods discussed above. The developing Communist, like all members of bourgeois society, is an open battleground between the alienated sides of his personality. Armed, however, with Marxism-Leninism, the prototype of the consciousness of a member of Communist society, he can, with the help of the Party, overcome this contradiction.

REDUCTIONISM

To the Communist, difficulties within the personality are obviously but the reflection of the contradictions of external material reality. They can be resolved only on the basis of a theory and practice directed towards the transformation of that material reality. Any outlook that considers them to be innate contradictions within the individual is a perversion of truth—"idealist," "mystical." For the Communist grants no independent existence to inner personal struggles. He sees them simply as distorted reflections of social reality.[5] Psychiatric efforts to resolve contradictions in the individual are not founded upon the idea of *overcoming* social contradictions; therefore, by the simple logic of practical Marxism, they are concerned with the *preservation* of social contradictions. Therefore, like idealism, they are weapons of the ruling class. It is this—and not primarily that the Party is afraid of betrayal of secrets—which is the true explanation of the inveterate hostility of the Party to psychotherapeutic treatment of its members. Its own "therapy," which is vital to its growth and strength, is directed to the destruction of the contradictions within the individual by merging him in the potential commune, the Party; and depth psychology is a serious intrusion of the "alien ideology" of the class enemy.[6]

Nevertheless, there is a certain curious similarity in one respect between Marxism and Freudianism: the "nothing but" type of approach. Derived perhaps from their common ancestry in the scientistic spirit of the 19th century, with its denial of an essential autonomous being to man, they both employ a somewhat similar reductive technique. The most complex reaches of the imaginative mind, the most delicate constructions of reason and of spiritual insight, become, for the practical purposes of the therapy, "nothing but" the play of the libido in *its* complicated figures or the play of class interest in *its* complicated figures.

In the Communist methodology this reductionism is of vital importance. The process of liquidating all unwanted traits, of developing the single eye, would be impossible without it. With it— granted the acceptance of the fundamental philosophical and political ideas of Marxism-Leninism—anything can be done that the Party deems necessary. Step by step, with equation after equation, the interest of the class enemy is identified with whatever idea, habit, or mode of living is to be eliminated, until the whole weight of a believed and accepted view of the world, the very meaning of existence for the Communist, is brought into the scales, directly weighed against that which is to be eradicated.

Despite its derivation from the complex, almost mystical Hegelo-Marxian doctrine of alienation, the operative Marxist psychological theory is extraordinarily simple. Men are the battleground between social forces and conscious understanding; and all psychological phenomena can be reduced to the effect of the one or the other. Either/or. Either you are with History and the proletariat or against them; and every act, every tendency, every trait, must be adjudged by this criterion.

COMMUNIST PSYCHOSURGERY

This implicit psychological theory is worked out in practice in Communist training as a whole; and that practice is, I hope, documented by the whole of this study, by what has gone before as well as by what follows. Nevertheless, it may be worth while at this point to give some idea of how this psychological approach functions where the problems upon which the Party acts are primarily non-political, and therefore more or less parallel to psychological conflicts in ordinary life. Seen thus in its purest form—although eccentric to its main and continuing function within the direct process of training—the operation of the Marxist-Leninist psychological method may stand out more clearly, since it is less involved with a political atmosphere of which most readers can have had no direct experience.

Such Party operations upon "personal problems" differ from the constant daily pressure of formal and informal training procedures in their crisis quality. They occur when a mode of the personality which has effectually survived the process of training is suddenly brought into sharp opposition to the Party. All the intervening layers which ordinarily mask such conflicts are stripped away. Either the interests of the Party for some reason demand that the issue be brought to a head before the normal process of development has "matured" the Communist through the erosion of "subjectivity," or the problem in question is of such a firmly entrenched neurotic quality that only a frontal attack can blast it out of the way.

It should be noted that, from the Party's point of view, it is irrelevant whether the conflict is caused by virtues—loyalty, attachment, love—which cut across the Party's demands, or by vices—alcoholism, personal violence, sexual perversion. The latter category may or may not interfere with Party demands, but they do endanger the Party, both by making the individual liable to indiscretion or subject to blackmail and by "exposing the Party to attack" on the basis of the individual's derelictions. But whether virtues or vices from a normal point of view, such actions and attitudes are "anti-Party," that is, evil and to be eradicated.

The treatment is drastic, and since it kills or cures, it is utilized only when the situation is extremely serious. But although it is not undertaken lightly, once decided upon, it is ruthlessly carried through. I have had experience directly or indirectly with a considerable number of such cases in my Party career, both in England and the United States, and I know of no instance where one of two results did not ensue: either the person was decisively transformed and jumped sharply forward in his Communist "development," or he left the Party—by expulsion or by a rapid drift away after "removal from responsibility," demotion.

The instances of which I had knowledge were widely diverse. There were those which, from any point of view but that of the Party, would be regarded as perfectly normal and indeed admirable: instances of devotion to father or mother, where the issue was one of time and energy involved in their material support or of time spent in attention to them; romances or marriages to be broken up because the promising Party force was allied with an "anti-Party element," or even a "non-Party element" (someone suspected of Trotskyism, or just an apolitical husband who wanted his wife to spend an occasional evening with him); deeply rooted remnants of "bourgeois" moral attitudes, taking the form of objection to participating in some piece of deception or character assassination or other skulduggery which the Party deemed immediately and vitally necessary.[7]

Then there were the situations where the problem from any point of view would be regarded as neurotic: a confirmed drunkard in his twenties who without ceasing to drink lost within a matter of weeks all the external personality traits of the alcoholic and became a powerful and effective leader of an extremely important movement; a girl of ability who at her menstrual periods collapsed completely and neglected her responsibilities—in the Party's view (and presumably correctly from the upshot), for reasons of "subjectivism"—and who, after a showdown, functioned perfectly normally; a homosexual who to all external appearances completely transformed his life to remain within the Party.

This last was perhaps the most remarkable and dramatic case of which I have knowledge; and since the process of direct attack upon a critically "anti-Party" attitude is the same in all situations, a discussion of it may illuminate the others. The approach in all such cases is delegated to a single individual of the leadership, preferably one who has been responsible for the Party work of the member concerned and knows him personally. In the discussion between them the issue is settled one way or the other. It may come eventually to a Control Commission, but the Control Commission simply registers the decision previously made by the leadership of the Party on the basis of the report of its operating member. The whole proceeding is in general conducted without emotional involvement or imputation of moral obloquy towards the specific character of the dereliction. The moral issue is—for or against the Party?

The case in point concerned a man of about 35, an outstanding member of his profession, holding positions of key importance in non-Party organizations. While not an open Communist, he was the recognized leader of the whole Left Wing grouping and a member of the "leading fraction" of the Party in the profession. As it turned out, he had been a practicing homosexual for many years. He had managed his life so discreetly that no hint of scandal had touched him; nor, during his five or six years in the Party, had any idea of his homosexuality reached the Party leadership.

A slip in that discretion, an advance made to a Party member, caused the crisis. The Party member concerned was neither hostile nor condemnatory; he simply felt that the situation was dangerous for the Party and reported it. The reaction in the District Office was immediate and unequivocal. A scandal involving the Party and jeopardizing all the work around Comrade H must be avoided at all costs. Only two alternatives were discussed: should he be expelled forthwith, or should an effort be made to save him for the Party on the basis of complete and immediate transformation of his life. The latter opinion prevailed, on the grounds of his capabilities and high degree of development; and I was given the task of "transmitting the decision" to him.

Comrade H was a developed Communist—or the decision would have been to expel him out of hand—and while my discussion with him was in no way hostile or brutal, it was sharp and direct. The Party, without taking any attitude morally or psychologically toward his homosexuality itself, found it politically impermissible. We recognized the difficulties in which he would find himself if he made the necessary effort to remain within the Party, but this was the only condition on which he could retain his membership. He must decide within two days whether he was willing completely to abandon homosexual practices or not. Otherwise he would be expelled from the Party. The Party would prefer it if, within a reasonable period of time, he married or showed obvious signs of an interest in women; but this was not essential. What *was* demanded was his Communist decision to cease homosexual activities. (It should be noted that with a person of his development, his word given to the Party was regarded as something in the nature of an oath. It is true, of course, that the Party could check up on him afterwards; but primarily it relied on his spoken acceptance of the decision, the pledge of his Communist will.)

Considering his understanding of Marxism-Leninism, Comrade H had probably long foreseen the possibility of a clash between his homosexuality and the Party. What arguments he put forward were feeble and soon abandoned: he had made an error of judgment, but in all the preceding years no such error had occurred, and he could guarantee that it would not occur again. To the answer that the risk was too great, he had no rejoinder. Very shortly he faced the stark alternative. Although he was tremendously upset emotionally, there was not a trace of resentment or anger against the Party.

What private hell he went through in the next two days I do not know; but when I met with him again forty-eight hours later, he had made his decision—for the Party. I knew him and worked with him over the next seven years. From every indication, he completely transformed his life. When I last saw him he was married to a very charming woman and was the father of two children, and he rose steadily in Party responsibility.

The method of dealing with Comrade H is typical of the handling of acute "personal problems" which the Party decides to treat radically. Where the problem concerned is a more socially acceptable one (and therefore, in the eyes of the person dealt with, not so clearly a danger to the Party) or where the "theoretical development" is not so great, more argument may perhaps be needed. Otherwise, the process is identical.

In cases such as these, the psychological theory of Communism expresses itself in its most naked form. But the same implicit psychological theory lies behind the whole process of the training of the Communist cadre. Timidity, the critical spirit, individualist resentment against authority—every personal trait which blocks the fusion of the personality in the mould of the Communist type—is slowly and steadily destroyed, but without crisis tactics or dramatic confrontation. To the degree that the developing Communist accepts Marxism-Leninism as a true view of reality, his acceptance becomes an anvil upon which his personality can be hammered into shape by the Party's constant blows against those attitudes which, by the technique of reductionism, are shown to be incompatible with the accepted Marxist-Leninist outlook.

From the Communist point of view, the entire process is conscious; and the major weapon in the transformation is the conscious mind. The type after which the personality is to be moulded is consciously determined on the basis of the needs of the Party. The theoretical outlook, which both vindicates the creation of that type and within the individual becomes the first prerequisite for its creation, has no concept whatever of the unconscious. The method of training itself, however much it may instinctively utilize underlying psychological realities, is based upon a theory which elevates to the decisive position the power of the conscious mind.[8]

A materialist Gnosticism—or a mystical scientism—Communism lives in the conviction that, having mastered the secrets of Necessity and History, power over nature and man is in its hands.

PART TWO

•

THE
PRACTICE
OF
COMMUNIST
TRAINING

SIX · RECRUITS

While it is true that a few people become members of the Communist cadre without ever having held formal membership in the Communist Party (operatives of various apparatuses or men in important public positions who have had direct clandestine contact with Communist leaders), normally the cadre is developed from members of the Communist Party. Therefore, typically, the process of the development of the Communist begins with recruitment into the Communist Party.

This recruitment is not a chance phenomenon. It is the end-product of many aspects of the work of the Party. Of course recruitment is not the single aim of all these modes of activity, but it is regarded as an important, perhaps as the decisive, index of their success. Everything converges toward this end: agitation and propaganda; mass actions; the quieter day-to-day activities in trade unions, other organizations and communities. "Recruiting" in the direct sense is the reaping of a prepared harvest.

Recruitment proper, therefore, does not begin with undifferentiated human beings. Two sets of factors have brought about distinct differentiation before that process occurs.

The first set consists of those factors which bring the individual within the reach of the Party. These influences are largely accidental from the Party's point of view, outside of its control: the political and ideological circumstances of the time; the particular situation in which the individual finds himself at a given moment; and, to a lesser degree (because the Party appeals to many different kinds of people), the personal character structure of the individual. The second set of factors consists of the actual subjective work of the Party: agitation, propaganda, activity. This further differentiates and prepares for recruitment those whom objective factors have brought within the Party's reach.

THE OBJECTIVE FACTORS

The first question, therefore, is: what combination of circumstances tends to make men susceptible to Communist influences? The primary consideration seems to be an ambient where, for one or another reason and to a greater or less degree, a mood of detachment from existing customs, attitudes, and institutions prevails, together with a hopeful or desperate openness to change. This is, of course, a not unusual mood in the 20th century, and therefore to a certain extent individuals anywhere and throughout this era reflect it.[1] More typically, however, it affects particular social groups at particular times. Consider, for example, the periods of important Party influence in the United States among two groups—workers, on the one hand, and intellectuals and professionals, on the other.

For the workers, three periods stand out: (1) the early

twenties, when in the mass-production industries and in megalopolitan New York the foreign-born workers, stimulated by the war-time disorganization of society and the Russian Revolution, surged out against the caste-like barriers about them; (2) the early years of the Depression, when the unemployed reacted to the shock of dispossession; (3) the mid-thirties, when a widespread movement of militancy and organization spread through great sections of hitherto unorganized American labor.

Among the intellectuals and professionals, similar peaks of accessibility are discernible. Some are contemporaneous with periods of worker accessibility and some are not. It would appear, however, that even when they are contemporaneous, different factors are responsible. Here the causes are primarily ideological—successive shock points in the disintegrative crisis of the moral and intellectual tradition of Western civilization in the 20th century: (1) the period directly after World War I, when the trauma of the first of the great modern wars interacted with a utopian glorification of the Russian Revolution; (2) the early years of the Depression, which shook the ideological and psychological underpinnings of the American intellectual as much as it threatened his economic status; (3) the decade 1936-1945, when the crusading spirit against fascism stirred the whole intellectual community—particularly during the Spanish Civil War and the World War II alliance with the Soviet Union.

The social ambient, however, is only a first condition of accessibility. A series of circumstances, some accidental, some essential to the individual, will determine whether he will be personally accessible, even if the general social preconditions exist.

Accidental are such circumstances as the strength and prevalence of Left Wing activity in the area, the industry, or the profession where the individual happens to be; the degree to which particular accidents of his personal history have developed responsibilities or interests in sufficient strength to counteract the impact of social forces; or, the mere chance of meeting a congenial associate, reading a book or a periodical, even picking up a leaflet.[2]

Essential are such circumstances as a firmly based religious faith or lack thereof; the character and strength of previously acquired ideological and political attitudes; or the degree of maturity attained by the individual, which is usually, but not always, a function of his age.

In considering the circumstances essential to the individual's accessibility, there remains the question of his personal character structure, his temperamental and psychological makeup. This, in my experience, plays no important part in determining the degree of accessibility. As in the process of training once within the Party, so in this earlier stage individual character structure does not seem to pre-determine the outcome one way or the other. It is relevant only to the *particular manner* in which the individual is affected and to the *variation in approach* therefore necessary to recruit him and to train him.

While the developed cadreman becomes very much of a single type, I found among the rank and file of the Party, as in the circles around the Party, approximately the same scatter of temperaments as in the general community. At the time, this was my general offhand observation; but in the years since, as I have read elaborate endeavors to explain Party membership in terms of specific psychological types, I have thought the matter over more carefully. By the light of every typology with which I am acquainted—Freudian, Adlerian, Jungian, neo-Freudian, Sheldonian, Riesmanian—my conclusion remains the same, that the distribution of types in the two Communist movements I knew best, the American and the British, was just about the same as in the world outside.[3]

THE SUBJECTIVE FACTORS

When the objective factors, social and personal, have differentiated the undifferentiated raw material and created a semi-processed stuff, the energy of the Party sets to work upon it. The two prongs of this attack are, on the one hand, agitation and propaganda and, on the other hand, involvement in activity.

Without "activity," in the Communist view, agitation and propaganda is arid. It is true that action alone is "reformist"; it may get results, ameliorate life, but it will not advance the consciousness of the participants. But agitation and propaganda alone is "sectarian." It may gratify the agitators and propagandists and convince a few scattered hearers, but it will never produce substantial results, because ideas can only move the recipient when they are unified in his experience with practice.

Nevertheless, the technique of agitation and propaganda is developed to a high degree not only because of the role it plays in the process of conditioning potential recruits, but also because it has at least two other functions to fulfill. At a more primitive level and when the circumstances are apt, it is a major weapon for the manipulation of masses who, though fundamentally alien to the influences of the Party, can be moved into action for temporary purposes. Likewise, at a more advanced level, these techniques have been utilized, since the transformation of the Parties into mass organizations, for the maintenance of leadership over the non-cadre elements of the Party itself.

Agitation and propaganda in Communist theory are formally

distinguished from one another. Agitation is "directed toward large numbers in order to achieve unity of action on a single question"—with the implication that rhetorical and emotional appeal is highly important. Propaganda is "directed more selectively to riper elements on a whole complex of issues in order to raise their political and ideological consciousness"—the implication is of more restrained argument affecting the understanding.

In practice, however, the separation between the two tends to be obliterated. In "sectarian" periods the weight of the line loads agitation on the simplest immediate issue with propaganda for the full Party program. Hence the dilemma of the Bronx landlord in the early thirties trying to surrender to a Tenants' Committee: "I'll paint the stairs, I'll fix the boiler, I'll lower the rent— but how can I defend the Chinese Soviets?" In broad periods, on the other hand, public propaganda for the full and true program of the Party becomes more and more absorbed in agitation for "united-front" objectives.

This latter tendency, towards the attrition of open propaganda, has in the years since the mid-thirties ceased to be periodic and become a permanent aspect of the Party's practice. The reasons are not hard to find. The late twenties and early thirties had seen the "bolshevization"—perhaps "Stalinization" would be the better word—of the International, the replacement of the leading role of the Party by the leading role of the cadre, and the transformation of the Parties themselves into little more than the highest form of "mass organization." Covert manipulation of the masses (as distinguished from open revolutionary leadership), which had always been a large element of Communist practice, became its exclusive content.

The total loyalty and dependability of the cadre has made it possible to maneuver with consummate ease. Kaleidoscopic activities on a hundred fronts—many of them seemingly unrelated, some of them even in apparent opposition one to another—are utilized by a leadership conscious of its aims and untrammeled by the congruence of the means, to achieve strategical and tactical ends.

To the degree that a shift of agitational slogans alienates one group, it becomes possible to work among another group. The cadre can pick up the necessary mass following for any wanted campaign quickly through an *ad hoc* front organization, writing off to profit and loss what it has left behind with the change of line. Many of those left behind will be there, as a matter of fact, to be picked up again when the negation is negated and the next tactical jog occurs.

RECRUITMENT PROPER

Because in this situation the burden of propaganda as distinguished from agitation falls largely upon the personal activity of individual Communists and upon informal activities organized specifically for this purpose (social events, discussion groups, etc.), the typical person close to the Party has consistently followed its line on immediate issue after immediate issue and has absorbed attitudes which have corroded the foundations of any counter-position he may once have held. But he is generally quite ignorant of the positive Communist position except in the broadest terms. In many cases he does not even know that the person he follows and admires is a Communist.

The problem of recruitment now becomes one of filling the nothingness which has been created in the realm of coherent ideas, and of polarizing towards the Party the emotional reactions which have become the common coin of his thinking on political and social matters. The stage has been carefully set.

As in the old shell game, the victim hasn't a chance. If he lifts the shell over this or that defense, it is always empty; the pea isn't there. It has been arranged that way over a period of time. All logic arising from the positions he has adopted, one by one, leads to acceptance of the Party's position. Intellectually he has no resources left for defense.

That, however, does not mean that recruiting is easy, even when the prospect is judged sufficiently ripe. Emotional factors will stand in the way; and then there are deep underlying rational attitudes which have been temporarily put by while the eager mind of the activist has accepted the specious logic of the existing situation. These have an uncomfortable way, for the Communist recruiter, of coming to the surface just at the key moment.

TECHNIQUES OF RECRUITMENT

Successful recruiting is almost always the result of direct personal work. Every Party member worth his salt keeps recruiting consciously to the fore in the "budget of tasks" which makes up his daily examination of conscience. The Party stresses regularity and consistency: "The important thing is to keep after your people constantly. Do it in a regular, organized manner. Haphazard methods never bring results. Keep checking on your prospects and keep following through!" [4]

Everyone with whom the Communist is in contact is, at a greater or less remove, a potential recruit. In the busy routine of activity this is always kept in mind; and all personal and social life that is not pure relaxation among Party comrades or a necessary toll of the external world should be geared to the end of immediate or eventual recruitment.

In the better-organized units this personal work is systematically directed and supervised. Long lists of contacts are maintained, sometimes divided into several catagories, depending
upon their closeness to the Party, with a certain number indicated for immediate intensive concentration, while others are,
for the time, to be worked on with less pressure. A portion of
every unit meeting is set aside for check-up on the member or
members responsible for these individuals and for a report of
progress. In units less highly organized, such discussion of "contacts" in specific terms is much more sporadic; in some it is left
largely to the initiative of the individual member until a "recruiting drive" comes along, when, under pressure from above, a
great flurry of activity takes place in order to attempt to fulfill
the quotas established for the drive.

The "drives" do little more than register personal work already done, work specifically shaped to the particular situation
of the prospective recruit.[5] The recruiter has to become a close
acquaintance, if possible a friend, of the person upon whom he
is working. What he says and does is based on thorough knowledge of the person and arises naturally from day-to-day inter-
course, avoiding the appearance of the arbitrary and artificial.
His approach moves from the particular to the general, starting
with the already accepted beliefs, the attitudes, and the personal
problems of the individual concerned; and introduces the Party
position slowly and gradually, step by step, as a development
which seems to arise naturally from analysis of that person's own
problems. Most of this will take place in the form of personal
conversation. Pamphlets, Marxist-Leninist classics, the Party
press, informal or organized discussion groups, Party-sponsored
classes are used primarily in the later stages and strictly as
ancillary to the central technique of personal discussion.

Furthermore, if the prospective recruit is not already active in some organization or campaign in which the Party is interested, it is regarded as of the utmost importance to involve him in one; if he is already involved, he must be further involved. Likewise he must be brought into social relations with other Party members or people close to the Party. He must be "drawn in." This experience, activity, and accustomedness are the anvil of "practice" upon which the hammer of "theory"—propaganda, persuasion, argument—strikes its blows.

The precise point at which the final pressures are applied to bring the prospect finally into the Party varies greatly from situation to situation and person to person. Where the recruitment is being carried on in a unit which functions in a conspiratorial or semi-conspiratorial manner, a much higher degree of "understanding" will be required before the recruiter is allowed by the unit to ask the prospect actually to join the Party. In more open branches, and particularly in more legal periods, much greater chances are taken; and the person's willingness to join on the basis of a general acceptance of the position of the Party is sufficient.

But, whenever it occurs, this is the crucial moment in the recruiting process. There seems to be an almost inevitable tendency on the part of potential recruits, with the exception of the very young and the very naive, to develop a reaction or block just at this stage. It may take any one of a number of forms —some newly discovered ideological disagreement or a criticism of a specific action of the Party or simply a general evasiveness. This is quite natural, of course; it is a phenomenon which has been noticed by those who have discussed other forms of conversion. It is not only a crucial, but a very dangerous time, from the Party's point of view. Those lost at this point can become almost as inimical to the Party as ex-Communists; or they can remain indefinitely as useful but cynical and critical sympathizers, whose potential for the Party is largely frittered away in a political no-man's-land.

Therefore, at this stage extraordinary efforts are made by the Party to assist the recruiter. Leading Party members are called in to help personally in conversation and discussion. This is the time for the liberal use of emotional methods, varying from the impact of large mass meetings to the flattery of inclusion in small and select social events with Party and fellow-traveling dignitaries, or in carefully stage-managed, almost-closed Party meetings, at which there are present only one or two non-members.

In my years in the Party, I had considerable experience both with direct recruits of my own and as a Party leader called in to assist with others' recruits. The problems I met with had extraordinary variety; the final block seems to have forms as multifarious as human character and experience, and very often it is hidden beneath a number of false "reasons," which must be disposed of before it comes to the surface.

Sometimes the attitude of a wife or a husband was the determining factor. The easiest—if not the quickest—solution in such situations was to recruit the other person, or at least neutralize him or her. Sometimes personal pique about the activities of some Party member working in the same field turned out to be the ultimate objection. To this problem there are three possible answers: either the two individuals can be brought together, under Party auspices, and their difficulties straightened out; or the new member can be assured, in a way which gives him a feeling of being already brought into the counsels of the Party, that the Party agrees with many of his criticisms, and in fact wants him as a member partly in order to overcome these weaknesses; or, if neither of these methods will work, it is sometimes necessary, and possible, to assure the prospective recruit that he will be given other more important work in another field.

Then there are an almost infinite variety of objections on theoretical grounds. If this is the real reason for hesitation and not simply a cover for some other objection, the only solution is to argue the matter out and convince the recruit—a process which may take a good long time and much effort, and which is by no means certain of success.

Finally, there are the large number of cases where the real difficulty is either deep underlying moral objections, of which the person is hardly aware himself, or a prudential regard for his future and the future of his family—what the Party would call "opportunism" or "fear." In such situations very rarely is it advisable even to admit the existence of the real reason. Instead, the objections actually brought forward are handled one by one; and meanwhile a combination of persuasion, pressure, and flattery is exercised. If the suspected reason is moral in character, tangential discussion of such questions, without in any way pointing them to the person concerned, is carefully induced. If the reason is assumed to be "fear," then in the same tangential way, reassurance is given the individual that the Party works very carefully, that all measures are taken "to protect members in special situations," that "progressives are safer in the Party than outside of it."

But, whatever the problem might be, there is almost certain to be a problem. Very rarely—even after the most carefully developed approach—is actual recruitment automatic. And the final clinching requires a skillful combination of pressure and tact.

The energy expended upon any single effort to recruit varies, of course, depending upon the Party's judgment of the probable usefulness of the individual. That judgment is influenced by two considerations. First, does the prospective recruit already hold some strategic position of influence or show signs of abilities which will enable him to achieve such a position? Secondly, has he qualities which indicate cadre-potentiality?

While these two possibilities may be combined in the same individual, it is the cadre-potentiality which is decisive. The ability to discern the existence of such potentiality in individuals who have as yet not been exposed to the Party moulding process is highly respected in the Party leadership. This ability depends upon a combination of experience and intuitive judgment, since no specific table of qualities or specification of types is applicable. Observing a number of potential recruits in the same activity or organization, one who looks as though he would be a headache for any disciplined organization of which he were a part can be seen to have precisely the qualities out of which a Communist can be made. Another who seems to have the most impressive native qualities of leadership can be seen offhand to be devoid of the inner toughness which can take the moulding process without cracking. A third who appears docile and hard-working would become extremely difficult, a real "personal problem," at any advanced level in the Party. And a fourth who because of timidity or self-effacement fails to stand out at all has exactly the qualities of character and intellect which in the training process will overcome his backwardness and make him an outstanding leader.

Although cadre-potentiality and strategic usefulness are the real criteria by which the Party leadership judges individual recruits, great emphasis is placed in Party exhortation and planning of recruiting drives upon statistical aspects. When quotas are placed for the country, for a district, for a section, or for a unit, the demand will be made for the recruitment of so many steelworkers, so many Negroes, so many "women in basic industry." In practice, the carrying out of such directives depends almost entirely upon whether or not the Party has carried out its "concentration work" in the areas concerned. The statistical "composition" of the recruiting, while it may be affected to a small degree by the pressure for "concentration recruiting," reflects little more than the previous activity of the Party. Judged by the real interest shown and the emphasis given in action, effective concentration in recruiting is upon individuals; effective discrimination in recruiting is between individuals.

And, in fact, it is those who have been the object of such concentration and such discrimination who turn out to be the sort of Party member with whom we are concerned—those from whom the cadre is developed. While there are a few exceptions among the indiscriminate harvest of agitational and accidental recruits, these are the good recruits, the stable and valuable ones.

Whatever finally motivates any serious recruit, and however weighty the factors of immediate activity and association may be, he comes into the Party because he accepts the Party. It is very rare indeed that someone joins on a single issue or the better to participate in a specific campaign, or for any such reason. A man joins the Communist Party because he wants to be a Communist, and the decisive step of joining the Party is taken with a deep awareness of passing a decisive climacteric.

It may be too dramatic to say that every recruit thinks in terms of a world abandoned and a world found—for familiar landmarks exist at one and the same time in the two worlds. But something of such a feeling imbues the decision: the hope of a clarity dimly envisaged but not as yet achieved; an outlook upon the world which will make petty, pressing problems sink into insignificance; the idea of action unhampered by the confusions of the individual stance; or the hope of being an accepted member of a history-chosen élite. It is, in a word—whatever the concrete content with which the peculiar outlook of the individual fills it—a decision of large proportions. Mean and petty motives, as in all human existence, undoubtedly affect it, but they are not fundamental.

Unfortunately, in spite of the naked power content of Communism, its public appeal is primarily directed not to narrow, but to broad and deep responses in the human personality.[6] And so, despite the fact that once a recruit is drawn into the Communist machine, terrific pressure is brought to bear to mould him into the desired ideal Communist by destroying his individuality, the process of recruiting itself concentrates upon him as an individual.

SEVEN · THE RANK AND FILE

Insofar as the rank-and-file members of the Party are not developed Communists, not members of the cadre, they must be led and guided rather as are close followers outside the Party, by methods of propaganda and agitation. On the other hand, since all Party members are potentially cadremen, the training of the rank and file must be directed towards developing as many as possible of them into true Communists.

The Communist leadership, therefore, is up against a continuing contradiction between two incompatible goals: the building of a mass Party and the moulding of an iron Party. Both are demanded by the oracles of the movement, and to attack either goal would be to be guilty of a deviation ("sectarian underestimation of the importance of the mass party" or "a rotten liberal attitude toward the membership"). In practice the dilemma is effectively resolved by varying the emphasis on "mass Party" or "iron Party" from one period to another, although even during the "broadest" periods the selection and training of the cadre receives major stress.

When the Party's tactics are "peaceful," "democratic," and non-revolutionary, widespread recruiting takes place; the new recruit and the rank and filer are put under less pressure; and relatively smaller numbers of the rank and file are subject to the process of cadre development. When the situation or the line changes, the emphasis is reversed. Recruiting is slowed; Party membership is squeezed, either by formal purges or by less dramatic methods; and the whole remaining membership is placed under much heavier pressure, with the aim of developing from the lessened number a much higher proportion for the cadre.

The enormously high "turnover" figures in Party membership —approaching as high as 80 per cent in the American Party over a five-year period in which I was intimately concerned with the problem, 1936-41 [1]—are the direct result of this process. There is constant complaint about "turnover" in Communist organizational discussion and constant criticism of the middle functionaries because of it. But "turnover" would seem to be a necessary result of Communist organizational and political methods. The primary aim is the creation of a steeled cadre, flexible enough to take any tactically desired stand on current questions, accreting strength as it moves through opposite and contradictory campaigns and feeds upon generation after generation of the rank and file of the formal Parties.

THE NEW MEMBER

Whatever the motivations and circumstances of the new member's recruitment may have been, however "theoretically prepared" he may be, he can have had little if any preparation for the life of a Party member. Even if he knows Party members intimately and has some idea of what sorts of things are demanded of them and of how their lives are occupied, he cannot have been in a position to grasp subjectively the quality of an experience so specific in character, an experience which is so radical a departure from ordinary life.

All circumstances emphasize the gulf which separates the new social situation from his previous life. Where the Party is well organized and functioning efficiently, the very process of his acceptance as a member is calculated to produce this effect. After he signs an application it will usually be a considerable time before he is notified of his acceptance, during which time the friend who recruited him is very likely, openly or covertly, to indicate that he is being investigated, considered, judged. Looking back on the weeks before he was asked to join, he may remember how much information about his personal history, connections, and attitudes has been carefully extracted from him. When he signed his application, his sponsor probably suggested, or even insisted, that he use a false name, and warned him not to tell anyone of his application. Thus, even before he has become a member, he is learning his first lessons in conspiracy—lessons significant as much for the attitude toward life which they inculcate as for their practical value.[2]

No matter how much he may have read or thought about revolution, whatever large heroic images of the embattled revolutionary may have presented themselves to him, he will hardly have envisaged the specific, somewhat petty and very immediate "outlaw" role which, in some degree at least, he is taking on. Yet, with that strange signature of a "Party name," he has already taken a small but unequivocal step towards transforming his loyalties to the accepted political authorities of society into disloyalties, and towards transferring his allegiance to a set of institutions with its own laws, its own customs, its own executive and judicial bodies.[3] It will be long before he can say with Dmitrov that the highest executive authority he recognizes is the Executive Committee of the Communist International and the highest judicial authority, the International Control Commission of the Communist International; but he has submitted his life, to a small degree, to the judgment of the bureau of a unit of the Party.

Very often, particularly if the unit he is to join is a shop or professional one, he will be personally looked over by a functionary, or even by the whole unit bureau. Here, the probing into his background and attitudes will be more direct and detailed. Here for the first time he is likely to experience that curious impersonal approach, amounting almost to brutality, with which the Communist examines an individual very much as a carpenter examines a piece of lumber.

It is not that warmth or enthusiasm is lacking in the immediate contact, but rather that the questions asked, the implied criteria, are alien to the immediate human situation within which they are asked. His family becomes a "social origin"; his race, his ancestry, his religion, a "national origin." Previously he has taken these for granted or found them a source of pride or a cause of difficulty. To his interrogators, however, they are but one more item in the specification of his technical usefulness, like the tensile strength of a bar of steel.

His ideas are of no interest in themselves; they are only important as an index of how "developed" he is. His occupation, his hobbies, his friends are but possibilities to be utilized. None of this will he realize fully: of some of it he will be entirely unconscious; but something of the tone is bound to penetrate and to add its weight to the other impressions he has been receiving.

After this preparation, the notification of his acceptance as a member of the Party and the invitation to his first Party meeting arouse portentous feelings. The sense of having taken a decisive step in life and the self-satisfaction at being accepted by an exclusive group are tempered by a certain feeling of trepidation before the unknown. He is splendidly prepared for the impact of his first Party meeting.

Unless it is one of those brief periods when the Party is behaving in the most "open" way, he will not even be told of the place of the meeting but will be conducted there by the man who recruited him or by someone else assigned to do so. Whether it is in a worker's kitchen, or a middle-class living room, or in one of those bare workers' halls belonging to one or another of the multifarious "language-group" organizations which dot the country, the circumstances of his induction will be much the same. Communist unit meetings, as a matter of fact, not only in varying social milieux in the United States, but, from my experience, in England, France, Germany, Holland, and Belgium as well, follow so similar a pattern that, except for differences of language and the details of local situation, one could be transported from Wedding to South Chicago, to Montparnasse, to Paddington, without noticing any fundamental change.

The general character of the meeting, apart from what concerns the new member personally, hits him all at once, a microcosm of what he is to experience in succeeding months. The very language used contains strange words like "Org.-Sec.," or "D. B.," and peculiar usages of ordinary words like "concrete" and "mobilize" and "sharply," [4] to say nothing of the formal appellation "Comrade," used here by people who have called each other by their first names for years. The linking of the pettiest problems of literature sale or signature collection with earth-shaking international and national events serves to transform the ordinary into the significant. In fact, perhaps the most impressive aspect of the meeting is the tremendous seriousness with which the proceedings are invested, not by explicit modes of speech but by the implicit attitude of the participants.

Apart from his astonishment at finding among the members people he has known but never suspected of being Communists, the transformation of personality and of role among others whom he knows adds to the impression of a world of trans-valued values. He will see a leader of his union or an influential person in his community taking a brow-beating—meekly or truculently or indignantly, but taking it—from the unit organizer or from some other leading member of the unit, whom he has previously been aware of only as a more or less insignificant figure. Or, if a representative of a higher echelon is present on some mission, the unquestioned authority with which he speaks—"The District Bureau thinks . . . ," "The Party's decision is . . ."—will teach him more about "democratic centralism" in one moment than everything he has read in a year.

Minor things strike his attention: peculiarities of Communist "parliamentary procedure," the prevalence of unanimity on any but the most trivial questions, the odd institution of "the summing up," all of which he will learn much more about later.

In this particular meeting he himself is a most important factor. He is a new member, and the others, as well as he, are affected by the significance of this fact. To the section or the district he is only an integer in statistical achievement. But to the unit, he is not only another step toward the fulfillment or the "over-fulfillment" of their recruiting quota, with the kudos that will entail. They also know him as a person, and the deeper emotional feelings, which from time to time become overlaid in the grinding trivia of day-to-day activity, come to the surface on such an occasion. Even before the meeting begins, the heartfelt greetings of those whom he already knows and the quick and intimate reception by those whom he does not know welcome

him to the "in-group." In the course of the meeting he is cere-
moniously introduced and the previous informal reception is
formalized. At one period he would stand before the unit and
gravely take this pledge:

I now take my place in the ranks of the Communist Party, the
Party of the working class. I take this solemn oath to give the best
that is in me to the service of my class. I pledge myself to spare no
effort in uniting the workers in militant struggle against fascism
and war. I pledge myself to work unsparingly in the unions, in the
shops, among the unemployed, to lead the struggles for the daily
needs of the masses. I solemnly pledge to take my place in the
forefront of the struggle for Negro rights; against Jim-Crowism and
lynching, against the chauvinist lies of the ruling class. I pledge
myself to rally the masses to defend the Soviet Union, the land of
victorious Socialism. I pledge myself to remain at all times a vigilant
and firm defender of the Leninist line of the Party, the only line
that insures the triumph of Soviet Power in the United States.[5]

At another time, when the line is different, the emphasis would
differ: for "Leninist" would be substituted "Marxist"; for "Soviet
Power," "Socialism." The language would be modified and more
"American." But the implied content of the pledge is the same.
Or, if it is a time when pledges are not the Party fashion, he
will be initiated with a sober speech by the unit organizer. In
any case the emphasis is the same: duty, responsibility, and
the privilege of being one of those who have elected for History
—or, to lower the tone, who "know the score," are not "confused," on the outside, dragged by events.

The details of his induction are no less conducive to this feeling of initiation into a new life. The Party card he receives from
the financial secretary, with that strange false name written on
it, is accompanied with a query about his income. Party dues
are proportionate to income; the bite can be very deep (and

this is only the beginning, as he will soon learn; contributions, literature purchases, subscriptions, mass-organization demands, will cut deeper and deeper, averaging from 15 to 30 per cent of the member's income).

What lies ahead for him is also adumbrated at this first meeting. He has listened to campaigns discussed and assignments made—and to "check-up," soon to become the persistent tracker of his steps. Now, however, only two evenings of the week are demanded: the weekly unit meeting and the New Members' Class, which he must attend weekly for four or six weeks. Of course, if he is already active in any organization, he is expected to continue that activity under Party guidance; and if he has an interest or hobby or a connection, the political value of which is immediately apparent, he may be "mobilized" on the spot to begin capitalizing on it—which will mean a further claim upon his time.

The new member's first Party meeting is the beginning of the inculcation of two attitudes which are essential to the being of the Communist: for the Communist, the Party is the be-all and the end-all of life, the center of all human purpose; and the Party demands of him no partial segment of his life but all of his life.[6] However nebulously these concepts may affect him at the moment, a process has begun which will continue for the rest of his Party life.

NEW MEMBERS' CLASSES

In the first few weeks of membership, the three most important influences are the unit meetings themselves, any activities the new recruit may be involved in, and the New Members' Classes. The particular form New Members' Classes should take is always a matter of considerable internal Party discussion. Clearly it is impossible in so brief a time, and with the pressing need of immediate orientation, to approach the minimum desideratum of understanding of Marxism-Leninism. Nor, on the other hand, are these classes supposed to substitute for what the unit itself should teach the new member about the details of practical activity. One central idea, however, dominates all the variations: to inculcate the desired attitude to the Party.

What follows is a typical set of topics around which such classes are organized:

1. *The Class Struggle.* This prologue is adapted to the level of understanding of the particular group. A capsule of the theory of historical materialism, it concentrates on preparing the ground for

2. *The Party.* In New Members' Classes, the Marxist-Leninist doctrine of the Party is projected primarily emotionally and imaginatively. The teachers are rarely regular teachers of the Party educational apparatus; they are selected from the most experienced *actives* available and encouraged to personalize their teaching from their own experiences and the folklore of the Party.

3. *The Organizational Structure and Methods of Work of the Party.* This is a delicate question for the new and inexperienced, and the wind is tempered to the shorn lamb. An idealized picture is presented, placing great stress on the theoretical existence of a flow from bottom to top as complement to the flow from top to bottom. Great play is made with apt anecdotes about the initiative of individuals, the wisdom of the leadership, and the "undemocratic" character of ordinary democratic methods.

4. *Analysis of the current situation and the current line,* with

renewed emphasis on the role of the Party and the particular
tasks facing the local organization.

Usually these classes end with a talk by some representative of
a higher echelon, a sort of second welcoming and initiation, in
which the personal responsibility of the new members is stressed.

Apart from the direct result achieved in these classes through
absorption of the material taught—the raising of the Party from
a mundane institution to a mystical entity—two other results
are attained. In the first place, the Communist method of teaching through a guided discussion directed toward a predetermined
end confirms the belief of the new member that the conclusions
to which he comes have been arrived at freely and by his own
thinking, although they always turn out to be the conclusions
of the Party. In the second place, another attitude, corollary to
this, is developed, an attitude without which the first would be
untenable—an enormous respect for the "science" of Marxism-
Leninism, both as an indispensable tool to be mastered by the
neophyte if he wants to become a good Communist and as
justification for the authority of the leadership. The leadership
is to be conceived of not in the normal democratic manner, but
as a board of scientists, the most capable Marxist-Leninists. It
is not their personal opinions, their judgments, that they are
putting forward, but their scientific analysis of the situation. It
would be as absurd to place the uninstructed will of the majority
of the Party against their judgment on political and social matters as to counterpose the vote of first-year physics students to
the considered opinion of a group of leading physicists. The
student emerges conditioned both to accept the decisions of
the leadership and to feel that, to the degree of his understanding, he has arrived at those decisions himself and will understand them more and more fully the more thoroughly he masters
the science of the movement.

THE RANK AND FILER

The experiences of the first few weeks of Party membership have a reasonably uniform character, and it has been possible to discuss this period more or less as a homogeneous whole. When it comes to a consideration of the influences which contribute to the training of the Party member throughout his rank-and-file period, a different approach is necessary. There is no assignable temporal order to the gamut of possible events. What may have tremendous influence on one rank and filer three months after he has joined may not happen to another for three years. And so much is going on at once in different areas of Party life that it is impossible to describe it except schematically. Therefore, I shall discuss *seriatim:*

1. The Party meeting: the focus of Party life.
2. The activities of the rank-and-file Party member: training exercises.
3. The impact of the Party in daily life.

There is a fourth, and very important category, formal training in Party classes, schools, etc. This will be treated in Chapter 9. It must be remembered, however, that throughout the process I am discussing, most members will be receiving some formal education of this kind.

THE PARTY MEETING

For the rank and filer, the Party meeting is the unit meeting. He may occasionally be present at a section convention or a section conference. If his unit has done some remarkable piece of work, he may even be shown off at a district convention or conference. But these are exceptions. The unit meeting is the point at which the rank and filer's Party life comes to focus. It is here that he receives the assignments which originate his activity, and here that he is held accountable for the results of that activity. Here he meets the authority of the Party and learns to accept it freely, through mimesis and through absorption of the universal rationale of Communist action, the justification of all actions in terms of Marxist-Leninist dogma.

The mode of procedure itself plays an important part in adapting the unit meeting to its dual purpose as an instrument of training and as a flexible means for directing and mobilizing the Party membership. The method of discussion and decision follows the uniform practice of the Party from top to bottom. In the unit bureau, the unit organizer, in the unit meeting a representative of the unit bureau, makes a report. The other members discuss it. The reporter summarizes, accepting some points in the discussion and rejecting others. His report, as amended by his summary, is adopted unanimously.[7] The only exception to this is on matters where the organizer implicitly waives his prerogative, and that he does only on matters of organizational detail or in preliminary discussion of questions of no "political" importance, that is, questions in no way involving the Party line.

This bald picture would seem to place the individual member in the position of an automaton, obeying orders without in any way contributing to the elaboration of policy or maintaining any feeling of freedom or initiative. But this does justice neither to the full situation nor to the subjective reaction of the individual. These discussions are often lively, spirited, and violent.

The illusion is sedulously fostered that this method gives the individual much more real participation in the making of decisions than a simple vote. A capable Communist leader of any level, whether he be a unit organizer or the General Secretary of the Party, will in his summary mention by name those whose proposals he adopts, and in rejecting other proposals, he will utilize his superior command of dialectics so that the rejection seems based not on individual judgment but on objective "scientific" analysis. On an important question, and in particular in higher bodies, to have one's proposal so adopted by the Party leader gives one a tremendous feeling of influencing policy and of personal achievement.

At any Party level, despite the risks of sticking to a position which is not approved, people fight furiously for their position—and are expected to. In fact, one of the commonest aphorisms of Communist morality is: "A good bolshevik fights for his position until the Party has made a decision." Of course, if he fights successfully enough to convince a large section of a lower organization to vote against the view of a higher organization, all hell breaks loose. Representatives from the higher committee attend a specially summoned meeting of the recalcitrant organization, after having individually called the leaders of the organization on the carpet. Not only the "incorrectness" of the decision taken, but the deep social factors in the personalities of the members which caused them to take it, are gone into at great length. And then, when the vote is taken and the higher organization upheld (as it always is), anyone who has voted against it, or abstained, or even opposed the position of the leadership in the discussion, is individually interviewed, patiently but inexorably, for weeks or even months. If he does not fall into line, he is disciplined and finally expelled. But here we get beyond the scope of this chapter. Such an experience is the beginning of initiation into the cadre. Those who survive it are well on their way.

Communist meetings, then, despite the earnestness and the comradeship, are extremely vociferous, even quarrelsome. Hardly a question is raised but arguments, more or less acrimonious, arise. Such an atmosphere, in conjunction with the inevitable unanimity at the end and with the constant pressure of Party authority, is well suited to help in producing that tension between personal initiative and acceptance of authority which is a desideratum of the developed Communist.

All agendas are thoroughly prepared by the unit bureau following an established pattern. The emphasis and content of the great majority of the items on that agenda are derived from written and verbal communications from higher echelons. Only questions of purely local concern are initiated by the bureau itself, and these also are under the over-all guidance of section and district. But the role of the bureau and its members in preparing reports is not an automatic one. They must take arid general directives and present them in a form which will stimulate the unit, interpret them in terms of practical activity for the unit, draw up a plan of campaign, and assign forces from their membership to carry it out.

The bureau is absolute lord of the agenda, and the agenda has tyrannical sway over the individual member. There is no such point on a Communist agenda as the conventional "New Business" or "General Welfare." The only way a member can place a question on the agenda is to discuss it with the organizer in advance. Then, if he and the bureau decide that it should be discussed, it is. Otherwise, it is almost impossible, without a small political revolt, to get it taken up.

The agenda of unit meetings has acquired through time a

uniformity of general content. These are the elements which are supposed to make up all unit agendas, and in the great majority of cases actually do:

1. The "educational"—a political discussion more or less theoretical in character.
2. The most important general campaigns of the Party at the time.
3. The most important activities specific to the unit.
4. Check-up on campaigns previously initiated and assignments previously made.
5. Perennial routine activity and check-up: Party press, literature, finances, etc.
6. Recruiting and discussion of individual contacts.

This is a tremendous order, and it is not surprising that the average weekly unit meeting lasts about four hours (except under illegal or semi-legal circumstances). It is a grueling weekly workout. No wonder the frequent complaint we hear from anti-Communist fighters in trade unions and other mass organizations that only the Communists stay to the end of meetings and decide the vote! They have plenty of practice. This staying power does not arise, as is so often implied, from the Communists' greater enthusiasm, but from their discipline *and* training.

In spite of the grinding, detailed character of so much of the business of the unit meeting, the recurring stress on theoretical considerations, which is a constant motif of the reports and discussions, has a cumulative effect. Even if the rank-and-file member does not get any formal Party schooling, he will pick up the essentials of the Communist outlook here. Very rapidly, phrases such as "bourgeois-democratic," "The Party is the vanguard of the working class," "opportunism," "petty-bourgeois attitudes," and even more esoteric ones like "tailism," "spontaneity," "left deviation," take on a content which makes them more than mere catchwords, so that they become connecting concepts in a developing over-all outlook.

In particular, the "educational" serves this function.[8] It is not a formal theoretical class, except in rare circumstances. At the time, for example, of a Party anniversary or the issuance of an important theoretical manual, the district will work out a series of outlines and send down special instructors to transform the educationals of the units into formal classes for a few weeks; but this is an exception. Normally, the educational is a discussion of some aspect of the Party line based on an authoritative contemporary Party statement and backed up with material from the Marxist classics. But it is predominantly *practical-*theoretical; it is concerned not with *developing* a theoretical foundation but with presenting, justifying, and building up enthusiasm for the political line of the Party.

The members are encouraged in the discussion to raise questions (if, for their "age and grade" in the movement, they are proportionately not too heretical); to bring up apt points from the classics to bolster the line; to suggest from their experience ways and means to implement it. The process is lively and at the same time cozy. The wolves may howl outside, but before the blazing fire of Marxism-Leninism, everything falls into comfortable order. No matter how little the rank-and-file member may be versed in the systematic theory of Communism, constant demonstration of the derivation of the Communist outlook from "Science"—that hallowed source of authority in our age—together with the feeling of solidarity in the fellowship of those who understand quickly prepares him to accept analyses and decisions of the Party as his own. Far from thinking himself subject to extraneous authority, he identifies himself with its conclusions with progressively less difficulty or resistance. He

considers himself infinitely superior to the "confused" and be-
nighted ordinary mortals who have to come to conclusions about
events without guide or compass, "blinded by the prejudices of
the capitalist world and drummed into sheep-like conformity
by the pounding of the capitalist press." Such justification and
acceptance of a series of minor changes, emphases, and de-em-
phases in the Party line "in accordance with the objective situation" results in a conditioning so effective that even among the
rank and file major shifts of line cause comparatively little
turmoil.

As the experience of the unit meetings develops acceptance
of the main outlines of Communist theory and of the leadership's
interpretation of that theory, so also it begins to create in the
rank-and-file Communist a new attitude towards himself. His
constant availability for assignment, irrespective of his personal
preferences, together with the constant check-up on his assignments, develops an awareness of accountability to an intense
degree. This is a situation in which no adult in a free society
finds himself. Everyone, of course, is accountable to someone
to some degree—in his job, for instance—but this is restricted
to limited aspects of his life. Even in the Army, whole areas of
life are free from discipline and constraint. In the Party, however, while the intensity increases only gradually as the rank
and filer moves towards the cadre, the pressure is always there,
affecting all aspects of his life.

A gradual displacement of apprehension of the self as pure
self begins, and the invasion of a new concept in which he begins
to accept himself more and more as a projection of the Party,
living and breathing only as informed by its spirit. Also affecting his conception of self is another phenomenon, experienced
mainly in unit meetings. He begins to conquer what the Party
calls his "subjectivity," to learn to criticize himself, or vote for

himself, as he would criticize or vote for someone else. Self-criticism and openly voting for one's self would be the two most strikingly bizarre characteristics of a Communist meeting to an outsider. But there is nothing self-conscious about these acts. From the very beginning the new member is habituated to the idea of a discussion of himself by others in the most impersonal way. Soon, by observation of what goes on in unit meetings, he becomes accustomed to the idea of people themselves participating in such a discussion about themselves, negatively and positively, though mainly negatively. If some of these discussions amaze him, the theory of self-criticism is explained to him by an older comrade.

Nevertheless, the first time the neophyte is himself subject to "self-criticism," it is probably the most painful thing that has ever happened to him.[9] For self-criticism consists in estimating (perhaps in connection with some failure of work or in consideration of promotion to some post) his own personality, his abilities and lack of abilities, and in digging into the circumstances of his political, social, and personal background which are "responsible" for his shortcomings. Of course, one is "helped" in this process; hence, the full name of the practice is "criticism and self-criticism." Part of the training is to learn to accept the bitterest attack as though it were impartial and impersonal assistance from the Party, and to join in the discussion, rebutting only what seems objectively untrue, emphasizing and expanding the rest.

Besides the function of the unit meeting in the development of Communist attitudes, it trains the rank-and-file member in many practical ways. Here he learns the painstaking methods of Communist organization. No matter how much organizational experience he may have had elsewhere, this is much more demanding, much more meticulous and thorough. A non-Communist organizer of many "cause committees," now an active anti-Communist, said to me recently, rather ruefully, that there were some advantages to the days when the "causes" for which he stood had Communist support and Communist workers in the ranks. "You didn't have to worry then about getting things done. They knew *how* to do them and they always *did* them. Now they're all like me—sometimes things get done and sometimes they don't." It is mainly in unit meetings that these skills and this responsibility are learned.

In the unit meetings also the elementary principles of conspiracy are absorbed. It becomes routine to call people only by first names, to communicate the place of meetings carefully, and verbally only, to learn not to ask questions about the sudden disappearance of a comrade from activity (when it is obviously not a case of backsliding), or for that matter not to ask questions about anything that is not one's direct concern. One learns not to keep written notes, never to write down names. One becomes accustomed to accepting from the tone of the organizer's introduction the authority of individuals present at the unit meeting without knowing who or what they are.

THE ACTIVITIES OF THE RANK-AND-FILE PARTY MEMBER

The relationship between the Party meeting and the activities of rank-and-file Communists can be looked at in two ways. If one thinks of the Party as an ordinary organization whose day-to-day and year-to-year activities are of primary importance, these activities would seem to be the *raison d'être* of the unit meeting. Sometimes, even in the Party, under the pressure of immediate events, it begins to look that way. But when that happens, it is because the Party is temporarily suffering from "revisionist tendencies."

The Party is not an ordinary organization; it is a special type of revolutionary organization, and everything it does in the period preliminary to a revolutionary situation must be justified by what it contributes to preparation for the seizure of power. So with all the Party's activities. They serve their purpose only to the degree that they "raise the consciousness of the workers," "build connections between the Party and the masses," and lead to the placing of Communists in influential and strategic positions.[10] But the main task of any Communist Party in the pre-revolutionary period is *to build and strengthen the Communist cadre* for the day when it will be needed for its only proper task. Any attitude which attaches value to activities for their own sake is, from the Marxist-Leninist point of view, reformist—that is, non-revolutionary, non-Communist, a "betrayal of the working class." It is the cardinal sin, revision of Marxism-Leninism.

Therefore, external activities must be regarded primarily as training maneuvers. They are subordinate to the inner life of the Party, and this is so despite all the emphasis on mass work in Communist documents. Certainly the Communist must be active, the Party must have connections with the masses, but only because it is no more possible to build a revolutionary army without the practice of political activity than it is to build a conventional army without the practice of field maneuvers.

In the training of the rank-and-file Communist, therefore, the activities in which he participates should be considered primarily in relation to the training he receives in the Party itself—in the unit meeting, in Party life generally, and in his formal education. Activities are the field in which he tries out his skills, both individually and in deployed formation; and the successes and failures of this activity become material for the analysis and discussion which further his training.

These activities are extraordinarily variform. There are straight Party campaigns: subscription drives and canvassing for the Party press; Party election campaigns (collecting of signatures, house-to-house canvassing, street-corner meetings, mass meetings, etc.); campaigns around indicted or imprisoned Party leaders; the selling of tickets for Party mass meetings. There is the duty of participating in demonstrations and picket lines, whether run in the name of the Party or of organizations and trade unions supported by the Party. There is the work of shoring up, supporting, and expanding Party-front organizations and of furthering their campaigns. There is the work within organizations and professional associations alien to the Party, neutral, or in the process of being captured. There is work within the trade unions and the factories. And then, there is the responsibility of making something of one's situation as an individual, whatever it is—in a profession, in a place of work, among friends, at a Brooklyn clambake or a Main Line dinner party.

In activity, qualities which are taught in the abstract within the Party are fully developed. Some of these are in the nature of skills: the ability to speak to small or moderately large groups; to run a mimeograph machine and write a simple leaflet; to subordinate one's egotism in personal contacts in order to achieve results for the Party; to thrust aside diverting and inessential conditions—from the point of view of the Party —and concentrate always on determined goals. One or two basic qualities also must be learned primarily in contact with the outside world. Fortitude, both moral and physical, is such a quality. The exercise of fortitude requires the presence of hostile forces, and in the activities of the Party there is plenty of opportunity for it. The rank and filer must have the moral courage to take an unpopular position among associates, friends, and family, or to put forward a minority position to a scornfully listening audience. He must be able to attack publicly a position which a week ago, "before the objective situation changed," he had defended just as vigorously, and he must be able to do so without the slightest thought that he is doing anything but a noble thing. He must have the physical courage to participate in demonstrations and picket lines where there is a possibility of a clash with hostile groups or with the police, or to distribute leaflets and collect signatures in tough and unfriendly neighborhoods.

Then, too, it is in activity, particularly where a number of Communists are well organized in a fraction within a mass organization or a trade union, that the rank and filer first begins to acquire a feeling of the power of the Party, a power with which he identifies himself. This feeling arises for the first time, perhaps, when he sees a half-dozen Communists, of whom he is one, carry out plans which have been worked out in detail beforehand in a fraction meeting, and bring an organization with hundreds or thousands of members to take exactly the position the Party wants it to take. This feeling becomes like the smell of powder to a cavalry horse. It consoles the Communist for many an external defeat and internal tongue-lashing; and the promise of its repetition on a greater and greater scale is a tremendous stimulus to the efforts necessary for his development to the cadre.

THE IMPACT OF THE PARTY IN DAILY LIFE

In the general life of the Party, in conversation, reminiscences, banter, this sense of the power of the Party is intensified by association with the victories of the international Communist movement. Partially through formal education and partially through reading Party publications, but mainly through the absorption of attitudes from older comrades and from the atmosphere around him, there grows an identification with "our heroic Chinese comrades," with "our glorious Soviet comrades, moving forward from the successful construction of Socialism to the building of Communism." The compelling power of this sense of grandeur is more than sufficient to make up for the personal difficulties and dangers in which the individual Communist may find himself. The cause is advancing, the chariot of History is rolling inexorably on, and the Communist is firmly seated on that chariot, no matter how uncomfortable his personal position.

In the great emotional mass meetings and in the songs of the movement this identification is ritually consecrated. The more popular literature of the movement, revolutionary novels, short stories, reportage—and Soviet films—contribute considerably. Conversations about national and international developments, reports on Party activities, pamphlets glorifying "the building of Socialism," all play their part in strengthening this identification with an advancing victorious force. The conviction grows that for the movement "there are no fortresses bolsheviks cannot conquer"; and the foundations are being laid within the personality of the rank and filer himself for the time when this slogan will possess him individually as well.

With the growth of enthusiasm and of the sentiment of comradeship towards those linked with him, he develops also a half-pleasurable, half-frightening sensation of bridge after bridge being burned behind him. Although this process, too, is only beginning and will not be consummated before the cadre stage, what is taking place are the first steps towards total commitment —what the Party means by "loyalty."

As he finds that the Party takes cognizance and demands an accounting not merely of his political activity, but of his personal life, his relations with his family, the books he reads, the pictures on his walls, the way he spends his vacation, of the casual phrases he utters, this sense of commitment grows upon him. And some day in gossip about some Party member who has "turned sour," he hears the phrase: "You can't resign, you can only be expelled." It is true, the Party in countries where it is not in power has no physical sanctions with which to enforce this anathema. But he has begun to understand what can happen even to a rank and filer of two or three years' standing whose life has become so intertwined with the Party that his friendships, his associations, perhaps his very career or job, can be blasted by an expulsion.[11] It is not that this threatening aspect is important to him at the time. *He* could never commit the sacrilege that Comrade X has committed; and the Party is fully justified in dealing summarily with those who endanger the cause of the future. Nevertheless, a gulf is created between him and the world around him.

The image of burned bridges is apt. Like Cortés and his little band in the midst of an alien empire, so the Communist, while he feels the strength of solidarity and of his mission, sees menacing forces around him everywhere. Previously, the policeman on the corner has been for him, as for most Americans or Englishmen, a neutral symbol at the worst, at the best a source of information and ultimate protection against robbers and other malefactors. Now he is transformed into an immediate symbol of danger, an agent of the enemy, the bourgeois state, with whom one's only potential relations are those of warfare. An alienation from the mores of the society is being artificially created. The state, from being the limited government of a constitutional republic, is becoming "the executive committee of the ruling class." Through theory, through atmosphere, through interpreted experience in demonstration or picket line, the sense of community with the nation is shattered. Very concretely, the idea of a commonwealth within the established commonwealth, and in bitter battle with it, is instilled.

The church is by definition the enemy of an organization whose theoretical basis is militantly materialist. The multifarious voluntary organizations of society, from Elks to Boy Scouts, have their parts to play in the "conspiracy of Wall Street." The "capitalist press" from being a paper to read becomes a direct organ of the same conspiracy. So with the family; and here more immediately because it is one's own family, and any relations with it which impede one's immediate usefulness and availability to the Party are directly and vigorously "handled." Nor is this merely a matter of filial piety. The intimate family, wife or husband, is included. If one or the other is not a Party member, all sorts of complications ensue, and failure to straighten out the situation by recruitment becomes a continuing and outstanding Party sin. If both are Party members, the Party assumes all sorts of rights to regulate relationships; family quarrels, the disposition of respective time, even the having of children, become political matters. At the cadre level, and occasionally before that, this has gone to the extreme of enforcing separation or divorce.

The most widespread, open, and blatant pressure of this kind on rank and filers that I know of in a legal Western party took place in the United States during World War II. Its aim was to prevent wives from visiting their husbands at Army training camps, and especially to prevent their moving to live nearby. Every political, ideological, and emotional stop was pulled, from sob-sister columns by Elizabeth Gurley Flynn in the *Daily Worker* to special classes for women, disciplinary actions, expulsions, and the threat of expulsion. The Party's motive in this campaign against what it indecently labeled "camp following" was to hold on to "female forces" to replace men drafted into the Army. To my personal knowledge, a number of divorces were precipitated as a result of this campaign.

In any individual case, the impingement of the Party on personal life will vary. In some cases, it may be a long time before important pressure of this kind directly affects the rank and filer. Nevertheless, he knows what the Party's attitude is, what his own attitude is supposed to be, and the awareness of commitment grows.

Commitment creates in turn a deep sense of separation from ordinary people, a sort of inner mark of Cain. Partly this is a feeling of superiority to the "confused" non-Party people around him. Partly it is a consciousness of always having another motive than the surface one, of living a special and infinitely more important life within the life he apparently leads. All affect drains out of situations irrelevant to the Party. This is the major reason why the Communist finds that he has gradually lost all close friendships with people outside of the Party. Communists —and this is true of rank and filers though even more so of the cadre—seem to find their really enjoyable recreation in informal, relaxed Party talk: talking shop, post-mortems, anecdotes, reminiscences, semi-theoretical argument, Party gossip. The drying up of personal connections of depth with the outside world is compensated to a considerable degree by the comradeship that undoubtedly exists in the Party, born of common association, shared perils, and the mutuality of sympathy engendered by a common ideology, a common loyalty, and a common sense of separation from the world around. This comradeship is, however, a different thing from friendship or love. While genuine friendships do exist in the Party, the comradeship of which I am speaking is less a direct relationship between two individuals, more a relationship mediated through the aura of emotion thrown up by the Party.

It is in this narrowing of the area of awareness of men as men, in this progressive depreciation of the value of personality, in this shifting of affect from real people and real situations to the Party and all it stands for, that the underlying source of the growing sense of separation is to be found. In the rank and filer the process is still in an embryonic stage; its further growth will bring him into the decisive area of rupture with the moral and spiritual outlook of his civilization.[12]

The Hellenic and Hebraic traditions of the dignity of the individual man, fused by Christianity in the self-sacrifice of a divine Person, imbue the deep consciousness of the West with that view of the human person as ultimately sacred which takes ethical form in the Golden Rule. Kant's expression of that ethic: "So act as to treat humanity, whether in thine own person or in that of any other, in every case as an end withal, never as means only" [13] brings sharply to a head the irreconcilable opposition between the native outlook of the rank and filer and that towards which he is being inexorably pressed. Very few men actually live always by this maxim; but most men in the West accept it in some form or other as the way they *ought* to live.

The whole of Communist training, however, drives towards the acceptance of the revolution as the end to which all things and all persons must be strictly subordinated as means. The Communist "practical imperative" would run: "So act as to treat the Revolution as the only end, and persons, whether thyself or others, as servants of that end." The good or evil in any situation is determined by whether it helps the revolution or impedes it.

Sooner or later, these opposing outlooks come seriously to grips. Throughout the Communist's rank-and-file experience, the development of such a crisis is adumbrated in smaller ways. But the crisis itself and its resolution will decide whether he leaves the Party, or remains in a suspended rank-and-file position, or moves to the cadre. Whatever secondary factors may exist in any individual case, the heart of that crisis is this clash of ethos.

EIGHT · THE CADRE

The training of the Communist goes on without ceasing until he dies; but training at the cadre level is qualitatively different from pre-cadre training in one important respect: the decisive role of *self*-imposition of pressure. The external pressures are still there and are even more ruthlessly applied when necessary, but the force of the Communist ethos has been absorbed into the personality itself. The pressures of Communist training seem to be transformed from objective to subjective forces, so that they are exercised very largely by the individual upon himself. The further development of a cadre Communist is therefore largely self-development.

That self-development is, indeed, heavily buttressed by the norms of his existence. The ways, prescribed by the Party milieu, in which he lives, carries out his responsibilities, faces his problems, and finds his satisfactions are of such a nature as to confirm his Communist "strengths" and put to shame his Communist "weaknesses." But the dynamic element is no longer "the Party," outside himself, but "the Party," bone of his bone and blood of his blood.

THE CADRE CRISIS

This transfer of the center of gravity of the complex of shaping forces from outside to within has been foreshadowed in the earlier development of the Communist. The occurrence of the decisive shift signalizes the transformation from a "promising force" to a "responsible Communist," a Communist of cadre quality. And, as each step forward in this direction in the earlier course of training is characterized by minor crises, any one of which creates the alternative of further Communist development or a "backward" movement, so this decisive moment of transition to the cadre personality is almost invariably characterized by a major crisis. The failure to resolve that crisis in Communist terms usually means its resolution in non-Communist (sometimes anti-Communist) terms—that is, either subsidence into comparative inactivity as a rank and filer or a more or less rapid dropping away from the Party.

The ideational content of such crises is essentially the clash of ethos I have discussed. Communists recognize this when they speak of "the necessity of choosing between two worlds." In fact, in many cases the Party deliberately raises an apparently trivial problem to a height which will create such a crisis.

While a clash of ethos is the ideational content of these crises, their emotional power is undoubtedly generated by the pressure to surrender the individuality of the personality, replacing it with the new Communist inner imperative. But since it is precisely the innate and unique value of the individual person which lies at the heart of the Western ethos, the ideational and emotional components of this crisis, in Western Communists at least, are interconnected in their essence. The crisis on all levels is a crisis of individual personality.

Sometimes the occasion of the crisis is an event of general significance, such as a sharp change of Party line or a dramatic challenge to accepted values; but it may just as well be some comparatively minor problem, the like of which has been met and "surmounted" a dozen times in the previous Party history of the person concerned. The point of development the particular Communist has reached, rather than the innate significance of the occasion, is what is important.

I am reminded of a young woman, a university teacher and practicing psychologist—a most capable "party force," both practically and theoretically, but far from a cadre position—who threw up her very promising career to go to Spain to supervise for the Party the administration of funds raised in America. She suffered hardship, lived under fire, and conducted herself with exemplary courage. When she came back, she turned down a number of tempting professional possibilities in order to become a secondary Party functionary on a district level.

The District leadership looked on it as a gamble. Despite her tested heroism, her capabilities, and her enthusiasm and sacrifice of personal opportunities, she was a long way from having achieved the sort of cadre personality which normally would be required of one filling her post. There remained too much individualism, impetuous personal self-confidence; but she was of old American stock (always a highly appreciated quality) and, by her lights, loyal. She had "pepper and salt," which properly channelized would be invaluable. It was a calculated risk.

Things went along smoothly for a few weeks until one day her superior—a member of the District Bureau, and, incidentally, a Negro—checking up on her department, called her to account because her records were not up to date. It was one of those instances where the Party demands the impossible. She had, of course, complete appreciation of the need for accuracy and tightness in such matters. She was not, however, used either to working without satisfactory assistance or to the fact that the Party demands achievement, whatever the circumstances, and acknowledgment of failure on the part of those responsible, no matter how reasonable the excuse. She flared up, talked about her previous accustomedness to having underlings take care of that kind of thing, and generally behaved in "a subjective manner."

For three or four weeks it was touch and go. The Personnel Commission was instructed to look around for a possible successor. There was a strained atmosphere when she came into the District headquarters. Then one day her superior came into my office smiling and said: "She'll do." Nothing dramatic had happened. From an external and objective point of view, all that might be said is that she had simmered down. But much more than that was involved. The expert eye of the Party leader had seen that a chasm had been crossed. What in Spain, amidst bombardment and shellfire, had been a romantically acceptable idea—that the Party demands everything, and failure is the individual's responsibility, not the Party's—had now been accepted permanently, integrally, and in the soberest day-to-day fashion. Even bookkeeping. And if bookkeeping for such a person, then everything else. The crisis had been surmounted. From then on her responsibilities were increased; she was accepted as a tested cadre person. That apparently minor incident, more than her sacrifice of a career or her heroism in war, had clinched the issue and served as the catalyst for a transformation of her personality.

All the other qualities are necessary; but granted everything—courage, initiative, "Marxist-Leninist understanding," qualities of leadership—a Communist is still not "tested" until his will has become fused with the will of the Party. And the test must perforce probe not the "strengths" but the "weaknesses" of the person concerned. For someone who is not courageous, it will involve questions of courage. For the naturally retiring, it will involve circumstances of flamboyance and excitement. For the person of large capabilities and large achievement, it will be based, as in this instance, upon drudging minutiae.

Sometimes the test comes upon a personal issue as large as the choice between going to a father's funeral or carrying out emergency Party responsibilities, or as small as an objection to working with a man who habitually ate raw onions. Instances come to mind as varied as fear of a physical clash; resentment at a decision made without participation where strict Party protocol would have indicated participation; or—where deeper moral issues were directly involved—responsibility for organizing a goon squad, for forging signatures, for rigging an expulsion, or for the immediate and unconditional carrying out of a sharp and unprincipled shift in the Party line.

Whatever the occasion of the crisis, however, the content inevitably involves a clash between personal judgment and Party judgment, carried to a point where the will is faced with the choice of which judgment is to be followed. And what makes the situation radically critical is the realization that this time, for some reason or other (presumably relevant to the characteristics and the accidents of development of the particular personality), the surrender of individuality is decisive. Final barriers are being crashed; the decision is not for this instance only, but for a whole life.

The demand for this conscious acceptance of the Party's will as one's own will brings about what might be called the "self-reversal syndrome," characteristic of so many cadre crises. The Party insists not only that a Party decision in opposition to the position of the individual Communist be accepted; but also that he who has made the "mistake" must become "the strongest fighter for the Party line." The pattern holds whether the problem concerned is an internal or an external situation: whether he is required merely to go before a Party organization and take a position opposite to that for which he has previously fought, or whether the same kind of action among outsiders is demanded. In either case the intellectual and psychological results are the same. To reverse one's self before other human beings, Party or non-Party, without losing one's self-respect, necessitates full inner acceptance of the rightfulness and power of the Party. For, "soul of a soulless universe" and god of a godless world, the Party idolatrously takes to itself the stance of God to Job: "Where wert thou when I laid the foundations of the earth? declare if thou hast understanding." Only by a god can such acceptance be demanded and only to a god can it be given without the utter destruction of self-respect. And this is the goal of the process: to force a transformation of the person in such a way as to preserve his necessary self-respect and at the same time make of him a loyal and driving microcosm of the Party.

Occasions of shift in the line give excellent opportunity for the Party to apply this procedure. These are what might be called natural or accidental occasions for "the self-reversal syndrome." But it is also eminently adapted to the artificial or Party-induced crisis. This is brought about when the Party has decided that an individual, or a group of individuals, have reached the point where their value depends upon their making the transition to the cadre. The risk is accepted that their failure to do so will drive them out of the Party altogether. Such decisions are taken particularly regarding intellectuals and those in positions of power in which the Party has placed them, for example, trade-union leaders; and at times when the hardening process is the order of the day, when the stress is upon "iron Party" rather than "mass Party."

In one way or another I have been involved in a number of such engineered "cleansings." One in particular, which I shall call the Thomas affair, may be worth relating, since it illustrates so many aspects of the process. A Party unit in the intellectual field—one from which the Party in the intervening years has reaped great harvests—had within it a number of people of obvious potential cadre quality. The District was satisfied with the work of the unit and the influence it had achieved in its field; but it was disturbed by what it called "anti-Party" and "anti-leadership" tendencies which from time to time exhibited themselves among its members. Not that they were not loyal, not that any "alien ideology" in overt form existed among them; but they criticized Party leaders, they criticized Party directives—and not in the accepted, off-the-record, griping fashion, but officially, in meetings. They even passed resolutions to be transmitted to higher authority, objecting to the use of certain Party leaders as speakers because of personal characteristics!

They were, in a word, capable, enthusiastic—and loyal, by their lights. The trouble was that the individualities of the capable, the loyal, the promising among them were not fully merged with the will of the Party. And even that could have been tolerated if this had been an ordinary unit, functioning well, able to be handled on any important question, led by average people. But the leading people were not average. A number of them were not only of potential cadre value, but also, because of their abilities and their professional achievements, headed towards positions where their "cadrefication," their absolute loyalty to the Party, was of the first importance.

Thomas was a typical member of the unit. His displays of

"individualist weaknesses" were not particularly worse than those of a number of others; by a series of accidents, however, some critical remarks he made came to the attention of the District Bureau and provided the opportunity they had been looking for to conduct a campaign of "bolshevization" in the unit. Called before a commission of the Bureau after a number of brushes with lower authorities, and faced with a set of demands—deliberately provocative—which no ordinary self-respecting man would put up with, he was goaded into statements which could be used as the basis for a decision expelling him from the Party.

While such decisions are often made by higher organs, formally the Party statutes provide that the unit to which a man belongs must expel him. Therefore, a full-dress meeting of the unit was called, with much previous "preparation" of the "more developed members" by representatives of the District. The members of the unit knew that Thomas's feeling for the Party was such that expulsion would shatter him. They also knew that most of them might have said the sort of things he had said and *they* were loyal Party members. Accordingly, the weighty indictment of Thomas by the District Bureau, complete with implications of concealed Trotskyism, of "serious danger to the Party," could not be emotionally convincing. The discussion which took place was heated and violent, and strongly pro-Thomas. In the end a vote for expulsion was secured only after a powerful speech by a representative of the District, who drew upon every resource—intellectual and emotional—of Party loyalty and concluded by equating a vote for the decision of the Bureau with loyalty to the Party, and a vote against it with a vote against the unity of the Party. The rights and wrongs of the case went by the board. The issue became one of willingness to suspend personal judgment, to subordinate it to the judgment of the Party leadership.

Nevertheless, although the expulsion was voted, a number of the most influential and promising leaders of the unit abstained. Abstention in a Party meeting is a recognized form of vote, but it is tabulated and taken note of. In some cases it is legitimate. In this case it distinctly was not. It did, however, give the District exactly what was wanted, an occasion for intense pressure upon the important abstainers, in order either to create cadre consciousness or to drive them out of the Party.

A battery of District leaders was assigned to carry out the most intensive personal discussion with them. The immediate aim was to secure a formal withdrawal of their abstentions, but in the course of the discussion it was expected that they would either be advanced tremendously towards the cadre or be so alienated that sooner or later they would drop out of the Party completely. These discussions, political, ideological, personal, emotional, sometimes went on for six or seven hours at a time—and repeatedly, a half-dozen times, if need be. The Party knew what was at stake and spared no pains.

The results in this particular campaign were "positive." One person dropped out of the Party in the course of it. The other four or five, in a formal meeting of the unit, changed their votes to votes for expulsion, seriously and sincerely explaining why they had been wrong in abstaining. Such an experience is decisive. The outlook and attitude of those concerned, their personality and mode of being, henceforth partook of the essence of the Communist. They were firmly on the cadre road.

In these cases, as in others like them, the issue between deep and decisive acceptance of Communism, on the one hand, and the beginning of a process leading toward total rejection of Communism, on the other, seems to be decided in each individual by factors so complex as to defy analysis. The Party's explanation, that those who fail its test do so because of "lack of sufficient Marxist-Leninist understanding," has certain elements of truth, but it clarifies very little. It simply pushes the question back one stage. Why, with two persons of apparently equal "understanding," does one react one way in such a crisis, the other, another? All that the Party explanation can mean, if it is to be more than tautological, is that either some unfortunate circumstance (when the crisis was accidental) or a misjudgment of timing (when it was deliberately precipitated) has occurred. Undoubtedly what takes place in the course of the crisis is a tremendous "leap" in "Marxist-Leninist understanding," that is, in full conscious acceptance of the demands of Communism on the person; but to determine why in apparently similar circumstances and with similar preparation this sometimes takes place and sometimes does not would require a study of the operation of psychological and ideological factors upon a considerable number of individuals in situations which of their very nature make such a study impossible. Whatever the deciding factors in the resolution of such crises are, however, the transition to the cadre inevitably seems to take such sharp and violent forms.

In fact, the whole process of Communist development is likely to consist of a series of minor crises, which are similar in character, differing from the cadre crisis proper only in their lesser intensity and in the lesser importance of the change involved. In the earlier stages, such crises frequently result in the rank and filer leaving the Party, either through expulsion or quietly dropping away. A positive resolution, however, does not have the significance of a positive resolution of the cadre crisis, because the person concerned is not ripe for so profound a transformation. It merely advances him a little further on the road of development.

Likewise, the further development of the cadre Communist

himself will be marked by a series of crises of a minor character. These take place, however, in people who have so thoroughly become Communist personalities that the resolution is
almost always a greater Communist "hardening" of the person.
The alternative—ceasing to be a Communist—has now become
unthinkable.[1] It may seem an exaggeration to say that the crises
which dot the development of cadre Communists have so one-
directional a character. Consider, however, how very small a
percentage of the seasoned Communists who have been through
the mill of bolshevization have broken with the Party.

TRANSITION TO THE CADRE

The transition to the cadre, and the crisis which accompanies it,
are clearly defined to objective analysis. But clear as they are
to observation, no sharp subjective recognition accompanies the
transition. This could not be otherwise in view of that undefined
status of the cadre discussed in the first chapter—its peculiar
combination of firm existence and lack of institutional expression. At the time, the person concerned may be gradually aware
of a new tone in the conversation of leading comrades with him;
he certainly will find a stiffening in his responsibilities; but these
things do not impinge on him in a dramatic way. Least of all is
the change in his inner outlook apparent to him. For a long
time he has thought of himself as a good Communist. The conflicts he has gone through during his recent crisis do not seemingly differ enough from what he has experienced previously for
him to recognize that he has undergone a profound change.
Only later in his life, with the experienced eye of the Communist
leader who has observed others and judged them, will he be

able to see the significance of this moment in his own development.

The life which lies ahead of him will change only by imperceptible stages from that which has gone before. Only slowly will he appreciate that he has acquired a certain élite position; that men who carry an aura of prestige treat him in a different way; that they involve him in an attitude towards the rank and file which is new to him. From the point of view of the leaders of the cadre, the change, though recognized, is not signalized. In their discussion of forces, his name comes up in a different context, on a higher level, than it did before. More is expected of him. He is less closely supervised, but criticism when it comes makes no allowances, is more savage, more direct, with the ideological explanations left out. This is not cynicism. Now he is expected to know them, to supply them for himself. He has passed his initiation, and, apart from any external pressure, he shares that inner sense of self-critical urgency which cadre Communists constantly communicate one to another.

One reason perhaps why the consciousness of change in status is not acute is that the emphasis on development and training continues with greater rather than less emphasis in the higher levels of the movement, so that there is a certain sense in which the feeling of being in a state of tutelage persists throughout a Communist's life. Whether this is so when one reaches the apex of power in the Political Bureau of the Communist Party of the Soviet Union, I do not know; but certainly I have found it as high as in National Secretaries of the Western Communist Parties—Browder, Pollitt, Thorez, Pieck—and in representatives of the Communist International—Ulbricht, Massey, Dmitrov—the highest level with which I have had personal experience.

TRAINING IN THE LIFE OF THE CADRE

While at the cadre level the primary responsibility for his further development rests upon the individual Communist, almost every aspect of his daily life and activity brings the power of the Party into play to provide both the opportunity for self-training and the external pressure to reinforce his Communist conscience. The fabric of existence provides occasion after occasion for training and testing: more dramatically in situations of inner-Party differences, at times of sharp change of the line or of external crisis; but just as materially in the routine fulfillment of tasks or in the solution of the petty problems which continually arise in every Party organization. One aspect of a good Communist's tone is the reduction of the dramatic to the commonplace and the raising of the commonplace to the significant, all meaning proceeding from the single total dynamic.

Everything is grist to the mill; yet all these outward manifestations serve merely as forms within which self-discipline acts, moving towards the goal of being so fully and wholly at one with the Party that its will is your will and your will is its will. It is, of course, the Party as an ideal concept, personified by the real Party but not totally coincident with it, to which this applies.[2] The most developed Communist can damn individual leaders, decisions, the state of affairs, up one side and down the other. He can be cynical, surly, violently critical—and frequently is. But he carries out with vigor and initiative every decision for which he is made responsible. Even when he most strongly disagrees with it, he carries it out firmly and of his own will, not with the feeling of external compulsion. The decision may be wrong, but it is right because it is a Party decision.[3] That which is the center of existence, his reason for being and the aim of all his action, demands that there be a Party, the aggregate of whose decisions are by its inherent character right. The aggregate must be carried out. If some decisions are wrong, to fail to carry them out would be to breach the overwhelming imperative that the aggregate must be carried out.

He will fight to the limit, at whatever level his position in the Party permits, against decisions with which he disagrees. If such decisions embody a trend, he will bide his time and fight again and again (it is possible, for instance, to discern in the history of a Party one knows well, individuals who have taken the same side of similar struggles ten, fifteen, twenty times, over twenty-five years—men who are perennially on the "right" or perennially on the "left," irrespective of which side wins in any given struggle). But none of this will in any fundamental way affect his fulfillment of these decisions. The Party has become a necessary condition for significant existence, and its constraints are felt not as constraints but as necessities which must be recognized and accepted in order that he may live fully and freely. Within that all-pervading atmosphere, criticism, cynicism, bitterness—all are possible, but they in no way change the fact that life under any other circumstances is unthinkable.

The general qualities of the Communist are sufficiently inculcated by the cadre stage that further training is largely a matter of the strengthening of already existing attitudes. It is becoming second nature to look at all problems of any kind instinctively and immediately in Marxist-Leninist terms; to accept responsibilities; to utilize the utmost initiative in carrying them out; to make of one's life an instrument of the Party line. These qualities are tested and strengthened every day. But that testing varies only in intensity from lower-level Communist experience, and since that has been described at some length previously, it would not be particularly valuable to discuss it again here. The specific quality of training at the cadre level arises from new forms of Communist existence which the new status presents, a new set of conflicts which have previously not existed to any significant degree.

These conflicts embody the contradiction between the demand that a bolshevik at one and the same time accept the most iron discipline and display the most independent initiative. It is true that this contradiction exists to some extent for the rank and filer. He, however, does not have the responsibility which makes the initiative he displays lead to consequences of importance.

At a time of sharp change in the Party line, for example, a great deal more is demanded of the cadre than of the rank and file. The non-cadre Communist, even if he is in a leadership position, can fulfill all that is expected of him if he supports the old position without foreboding or premonition, even with increasing intensity, right up to the change; goes through a few days' questioning and crisis at that time; and emerges in full support of the new position.

For the cadre Communist the situation is not so simple. He is speaking, he is teaching, he is answering the questions of Party rank and filers and of non-Party people; he is discussing and arguing extensions, perspectives, innuendoes of the line with his peers. Of course, on none of these occasions can he throw doubt upon the existing line, but much of his prestige in the future will depend upon the way in which at this time he avoids making mistakes (from the point of view of the future). He must be able to discuss what is coming with Marxist-Leninist sagacity; accept what exists at the moment with the fortitude of Communist discipline; and avoid at all costs the reputation of being an "opportunist," a trimmer.

A few vignettes of incidents at the time of two sharp changes of line—June 1941 and August 1939—may serve to illustrate and clarify. All the participants in these incidents were distinctly of cadre status, functioning at this time in the official Party organization as leaders of an important district.

In 1941, some months before the Hitler invasion of the Soviet Union, during a speculative conversation with a number of other leading comrades, Comrade A threw out the idea that the then current line of opposition to "Anglo-French imperialism and Roosevelt's war policy" might very possibly be extended into something like the Popular Front of the previous period. A united front with German Fascism internationally and with isolationist groups in America nationally might be formed. It is true that tentative proposals of attempting to infiltrate America First, particularly "from below," had already been broached in the Party, but Comrade A developed his ideas thoroughly and theoretically. There was considerable discussion and disagreement on the part of the others in the conversation; nothing more eventuated, except that from time to time during the next few weeks he casually returned to his concepts in conversation. No one took them too seriously—but they were possibilities to be considered.

When a few months later, with the invasion of the Soviet Union by Hitler, the line sharply changed, he fully and enthusiastically went along with it. Had he shown some prescience of the sharp transformation which actually occurred, it would have redounded positively to his credit. But the extreme versions of the previous line which he had projected in this speculative manner were never in any sense held against him. They had never been put forward as a criticism of the existing Party position, but merely as an imaginative projection of possible developments in the world situation as it then looked from the Communist point of view.

On the other hand, Comrade B a few months before the Nazi-Soviet pact showed great prescience of the future—and dealt a severe blow to his prestige and position in the cadre in the course of doing so. Analyzing the development of events and interpreting Stalin's speech at the 1938 Congress of the Communist Party of the Soviet Union, he correctly foresaw the end of the Popular Front line, and said so. Although he did not attack that line or the Party's judgment in continuing it, his whole tone was emotional, upset, worried. The net result was to imply lack of confidence in the existing line. That is all: but that very tone weighed heavily against him; it was enough to cause mentally raised eyebrows and to create around him an attitude of questioning. And even when events bore him out, the fact that he had been "correct," that he had taken a position which turned out to be an accurate forecast of the line, did him no good at all. The style of his discourse simply did not reflect the level of "understanding" he was supposed to have.

In both cases it was the tone, the attitude, which was decisive, irrespective of the "correctness" of the judgment. At first sight, therefore, the conclusion might be drawn that the safest thing to do is to keep your mouth shut. But one who reacts that way does not in general get very far, because he soon gets a reputation for being timid, weak, opportunist. He is not, by definition, a very promising cadre Communist. The pressures of emulation of the Communist type, both self-imposed and imposed by the mores of the movement, are exerted as strongly to create initiative and willingness to take a position as they are to bring about unquestionable faithfulness to the Party.

From the Communist point of view, it is not what you say but what you think, consciously or even half-consciously, that is important. If you think it, you should say it. A cadreman might be defined as a Communist in whom the complex internal pressures are such that, on the whole, he does say it; just as the mechanisms of Party training are designed all the way along to make sure that he says it. The "better" he is, the more he does say it; but, at the same time, the more his faithfulness to the Party increases, so that neither what he thinks nor what he says ever implies the slightest shadow of a doubt as to his deep loyalty.

Let me illustrate from the attitude of Comrade C, the District Organizer, a powerful veteran with international standing. During the summer before the Nazi-Soviet Pact, the newspapers were full of rumors of an impending *rapprochement* between Russia and Germany. The general Party reaction, of course, was, "slanders of the bourgeois press"; and this was certainly the official public point of view of the Party. But when Communists in internal conversation displayed the same emotional tone and the same certainty that the rumors must be lies, Comrade C reacted very sharply. Not that he denied that anything the capitalist press said was ill-intentioned and slanderous, or that he took any exception to the existing line, or even assumed that there was any great probability of a change in line in the immediate future. But he was highly critical both of the carrying over of agitational emotion into sober Communist appraisal and of inflexible insistence on what was, after all, only the current line, not a fundamental doctrinal truth.

His prestige, already very high, was heightened by these exchanges, but this was not because the rumors were actually true and he had to some degree foreshadowed the change of line which occurred shortly afterward. It arose, rather, from the combination of his ability to apply Communist principles, unaffected by the slogans of the moment, and his complete acceptance of the practical line those slogans reflected—an acceptance which his words and actions made clear was not merely acceptance of the line in a practical sense but as Truth, in that it was the line of the Party.

These incidents may in their contrast show something of the content of the conflict within the cadre Communist. They all arose out of the informal discussion which constantly goes on among leading Communists. Other incidents, equally relevant to the exertion of pressure and the tempering of the Communist personality, arise in every sphere of cadre life: in organizational work; in speaking, teaching, and writing; in disciplinary actions and in control commissions; in leading bureaus, committees, and in conventions; and, more formally, in the intensive circumstances of the high-level Party training-schools—district, national, and international.

Regarded from the point of view of behavior, the all-pervasive pressure on the Communist cadre can best be described in terms of his extreme care (however embracing or picayune the question under consideration) in choosing ideas, words, tone. This is "formulation." While "correct formulation" is always vital, it is at the periodic formal moments of Party life—in District and National committee meetings and conventions—that the ability to participate in the stylized "discussion" of such events, with the precisely correct feel, is scrutinized most minutely as an index of development. It is necessary, of course, that good work shall have been done by the person concerned in order that his "contribution to the discussion" will raise his prestige or maintain his position; but the work itself will profit him little unless it becomes the foundation from which he "draws the proper conclusions," "linking them up" with the major report, with just the right addition of original ideas to make his acceptance of the main line deeply personal, not a lifeless, mechanical echo.

The procedure of such committees and conventions, like all formal Communist policy meetings, takes the form of a discussion around a major report by the leader of the organization, which, with his summary at the end, is condensed into a series of resolutions which are unanimously adopted. Within the unanimity with which each participant in the discussion signalizes the virtues of the main report, however, serious differences (from the Communist point of view) can be expressed. At a second remove, as mysterious to the uninformed observer as the circling motions of tomcats in the elaborate ritual of their nocturnal meetings, the most daring of challenges, and sometimes the gravest of inadvertent blunders, take place—momentary events which make or mar a career.

These phenomena might seem to have little to do with training in the largely self-implemented form which is characteristic of it at the cadre level. It might seem that with a little experience the accepted pattern could be imitated without its necessarily demanding inner "understanding." I have, however, observed too many try it to believe that it can be done—either those too limited to rise above the lowest level of the cadre or leaders of the official Party who had for one reason or another reached their position but had never been cadre Communists at all. "Phrasemongering" is unerringly detected, and elicits blistering invective or is tolerantly ignored in a hum of inattention—according to the motives imputed.

Since no one can search the inner motivations of men, and since history shows all kinds of inspired opportunists to have existed, it is impossible to make a categorical statement that will cover absolutely all cases. Such possible exceptions aside, however, the attainment of the true Communist tone requires a balance derived from inner understanding and acceptance. The ordeal of the committee and the convention, and all the other rituals of Communist life, are for the cadre Communist but testings and measures. In that respect they serve an important function in his training, but the dynamic process occurs within him. If he has not there achieved the proper balance between the contradictories demanded of him, nothing he can do at the moment of assay, however shrewd and capable he may be, can simulate it.

"SELF-CRITICISM," "SUBJECTIVITY," "OBJECTIVITY"

Of course, the constant observation of others acting in a cadre manner and the continuing expectation that one will oneself live up to such standards exercise an external pressure complementary to the internal subjective pressure. At this stage the external processes are hardly felt as pressure. The subjective acceptance of Communist modes of existence has gone so deep that the punishment which every leading Communist takes day after day is hardly more noticed, sustained as the personality is by the stiffening of the subjective self-pressure, than is the external pressure of the earth's atmosphere upon the body. This is the way things are. This is the form of Communist being.

Therefore, "criticism and self-criticism" becomes, in a way it can never be for the rank and filer, a natural approach, a habit. It approximates what it is supposed to be in the ideal image put forward in Communist literature—a mode of looking at things devoid of concern for self. Men being what they are, such an ideal obviously is never completely realized. Personal interests —if in no other terms than one's own department or organization versus more general interests of the Party—impinge and affect judgment. But to a remarkable degree that ideal is realized in the seasoned cadre Communist. He takes what anywhere else would be regarded as unmitigated abuse, and hands it out as necessary, with extraordinarily little of the emotions of abasement or resentment, on the one hand, or aggressive ego-satisfaction, on the other. Either of these—"breast-beating" or "a rotten bureaucratic attitude toward the membership"—is a recognized weakness, extremely serious if any tendency towards it shows up in a member of the cadre, particularly serious, in fact, because it indicates "lack of self-criticism."

It is not that people do not feel personal chagrin at failure and pride at achievement. But this cannot be allowed to interfere with judgment, or to shadow to the faintest degree the fundamental criterion of the *Party's* success or failure in a given situation. To be politely modest on one of the rare occasions of Party praise would be considered as grave a shortcoming as to resent criticism or to pour out immoderate self-abnegation ("to beat one's breast") on the much more frequent occasions of blame. Anything of this sort is "subjectivity."

And subjectivity is the cardinal sin. "Subjectivity" is the climax of every condemnation—formal or informal. Whether the charge is "dereliction of duty," or "endangering the safety of the Party," or ideological deviation, the bill of particulars fuses into a single indictment: placing personal considerations above the interests of the Party, subjectivity. That such personal interest might from any non-Communist point of view be regarded as the sheerest altruism—truth, ethical considerations, love or friendship—is irrelevant. To put anything whatever before the Party is subjectivity.[4]

As "subjectivity" is the cardinal sin, its opposite, "objectivity," which amounts to neither less nor more than unconditional devotion to the Party, is the cardinal virtue. All the other virtues of the Communist are encompassed in this; and it is this which provides the ground for the resolution of the contradiction between the demand for independent initiative and the demand for iron discipline. Only in the identification of self with Party is it possible for two such opposites to exist with equal strength in the same personality; and towards the absolute establishment of that identity the inner pressure of the developed Communist personality, buttressed by the norms of Communist life, is directed.

The "deepening of Marxist-Leninist understanding," which is a major responsibility of the cadre Communist, broadens and intensifies the intellectual certainty that the Party stands for everything true and real in the objective world. Experience daily "proves" that only in utter identification with the Party, in uncompromising devotion to it, can the demands that are made upon him and that he makes upon himself, be reconciled. The real proving-ground—both exercise and test—of the bolshevik will lies in the steadfast holding to this pole, rather than in "courage in the face of the class enemy" or "resolute determination to overcome all obstacles," which are the common coin of the literature on this question.

The Party being in actuality the creature of the rulers of the Soviet Union, this devotion is, in grim literalness, devotion to their interests. But although this is vitally important in assessing the significance of Communism and the action of Communists from the practical standpoint, the ideational image and emotional focus towards which the devotion of the Communist personality directs itself remains not the Soviet Union and its leaders, but "the Party." Certainly, "the first duty of Communists is the defence of the Soviet Union"; certainly, "the Soviet Union is the touchstone of all political questions," the "socialist fatherland," "the stronghold of world Communism"; but the Soviet Union is subsumed, as it were, under the greater symbol of the Party. The faith triumphant, the Soviet Union, is still but an aspect of the faith. It is the faith, whole and entire, Communism, the Party, which inspires the Communist's universe and is the object of his devotion.[5]

That is why the known realities of the Soviet Union—oppression, slave-labor camps, purge after purge, murder in the millions, brutal and unprovoked aggression, even Khrushchev's exposure of Stalin and the Hungarian Revolution of 1956—slide off the cadre Communist's conscience like water off a duck's back. They make no live impact upon him. Intellectually he explains them as necessary casualties of the historic process, unfortunate but unavoidable. Emotionally they simply are not real, even when he has actually seen horrors with his own eyes. Facts that do not fit the theoretical outlook of Marxism-Leninism have only a shadowy existence. Reality rests only in the doctrines of Communism and the institution of the Party.[6]

If ever a trained and developed cadre Communist allows himself fully and deeply to acknowledge any reality independent of the Communist cosmos—a fact, an idea, an aspect of an order of being—the whole tense, complex structure is in imminent danger of shattering into bits. Only the most stupendous and immediate effort of the will can close the breach. The man to whom this is happening sometimes pretends to himself that he does not recognize its significance; but in such cases, almost always the Party smells it. Then, if he admits it, to the Party and to himself, everything possible is done to help him make that effort of will. But if he denies it, he is boxed off, trapped into compromising or blackmailable situations, demoted, expelled, vilified. For, even if *he* does not know that he has taken the first step on the road out of the Party, which for a cadre Communist means the road to hostility towards the Party (the Party speaks of "the iron law of renegacy"), the Party does, and it will stop at nothing to neutralize the threat.[7]

Whatever the circumstances, however, alone with himself or under the pressure of the most intensive Party effort, any breach whatsoever in the structure of Communist belief must be closed the moment it opens or the whole structure collapses. It is not strange that this should be so. The complex outlook of Marxism-Leninism creates so sharp a contrast with the empirically observable world and with the inherited ethos of the West, the strain upon the man who accepts it with the depth and whole-heartedness of a cadre Communist is so great, the tensions within the personality are held at so taut a pitch, that its very unity is its weakness, once it is pierced at any point. Or, to change the metaphor, the Communist personality is like that transparent sphere of legend which no sword or axe could mar, but which flew apart in a thousand pieces at the playing of the right note of music.

To very few among the thousands of cadre Communists of the Western Parties does this occur.[8] In the American Party I do not know of a score of cadre Communists who have broken within the last twenty years and this despite the serious crises which beset it in 1945 and 1956. It seems to require a most unusual set of circumstances to penetrate the powerful defenses of the Communist personality at this level of development. What is it then that ever brings about that irretrievable moment when reality makes itself felt so deeply that it cannot be repelled? To answer this question is difficult, for such events occur in the recesses of men's souls. But I shall hazard some generalizations based upon my own experience and what I have heard and read of the experience of others.[9]

Two prior conditions, I believe, must be fulfilled before the moment of acceptance of a reality counter to the Communist outlook is possible. First, there must have been over a considerable period of time a continuing series of doubts and questions, quickly repressed, but not fully dealt with and intellectually overcome, so that they have, if only to a small degree, sapped and weakened the foundations of Marxist-Leninist belief. Such a substratum, however, is not by itself a sufficient pre-condition. Secondly, there must occur some separation of the person from the Party, geographically or emotionally, for a time. Whittaker Chambers speaks of the susceptibility of one "in prison, in illness, in indecision." In my own case it was separation from the all-pervasive pressure of the Communist movement during service in the Army. In his case, Chambers indicates the emotional impact of an infant daughter on him.

But, though these are pre-conditions, they are not certain cause. Many have had their suppressed doubts, have suffered isolation "in prison, in illness, in indecision," without a break in their Communist defenses. Only a very few have found their pre-existing doubts welling up so strongly that at some point they recognized with a power that could not be denied that something was true and real which, by its truth and reality, shattered the foundations on which their life was built. Why many react one way and a few another, I do not know. The personal factors involved are too complex, and those who have broken vary too greatly in background and character, to make any final judgment.

One thing, however, is certain. So strong is the impress of the Communist mould, that to follow the path upon which they then find themselves compelled to proceed is not an easy, quick, or automatic process. It is, in fact, a "dark night of the soul," mentally and spiritually agonizing to a degree which makes the extreme personal and social difficulties which the Party creates for them seem minor. Perhaps a premonition of this—a horror of the void through which one must pass before finding a new understanding on the other side—is an additional buttress to the Communist will in resisting the temptations of reality and truth. For it is the will which decides the issue. Exerted steadfastly day by day—because doubt after doubt creeps in and must be dealt with—it is called to its supreme effort when some eventuality creates the conditions in which the threat to long-accepted certainties arises.

But the will does not function in a vacuum. The Communists say, when a defection occurs at a high level, that the person concerned "never fully understood and accepted Marxism-Leninism." They find indications in all his writings, his speeches, his actions, to prove their contention. It may well be that in the deepest sense they are right. The cadre Communist who breaks has retained somewhere within his personality values, elements of understanding, which are alien to the world-view of Marxism-Leninism.

The bolshevik will is decisive to the Communist personality. But that will is founded upon a deeper stratum. It is founded on belief, intellectual and emotional, in the truth of the Marxist-Leninist ideology, of which the Party is the living expression. Devotion to the Party, like the will to resist all challenges to that devotion, rests in the end on belief.

NINE · PARTY TRAINING SCHOOLS

The decisive factor in the moulding of the Communist is the impregnation of his consciousness with the set of concepts that make up the Communist world-view, the intellectual framework of the structure of Communist belief. The indoctrination of these concepts is a process which depends, as I have tried to show, not on formal instruction alone or even primarily, but on the sum of pressures which are continuously exerted upon the Communist at all stages of his development.

Formal instruction, however, although it is neither the sole nor the primary engine of transformation and training, has nevertheless a unique place in the training process and in the hierarchy of the sacred values of the Party. It is not primary, but it is in a sense ultimate in the Party's myth of the odyssey of the Communist. For it is in the inner schools of the Party that the experience of the developing Communist is brought to incandescent summation. Or, to change the metaphor, the schools he attends at the several stages of his career represent each an initiation into a new level of responsibility and authority in the cadre.

RANK-AND-FILE SCHOOLS AND CLASSES

It is with these cadre schools that this chapter is essentially concerned. But before discussing them, a word may be in order about schools and classes for the rank and file. Something of the aura that surrounds the cadre schools, the numinous attitude towards them, spills over into the formal classes which are held for rank-and-file Communists, and even into the more theoretical courses conducted in "open" schools of the Workers-School or Jefferson-School type, in especial when attendance there is placed upon the Communist as a Party "assignment," a Party duty. The content of these courses—whether inner-Party or open—parallels in general the content of the teaching of the cadre schools; something of the methods of teaching of these schools is followed, though in a much modulated manner; and the half-rational, half-mystical authority of the teacher in the cadre schools is reflected with lower intensity in the teacher of every Party course, whatever its level.

At the rank-and-file level, however, just as the pressure upon the Communist in his day-to-day activities is mild when compared to the similar pressure upon the developing cadreman, so the intensity of formal Communist schooling is a dim reflection of the force that is brought to bear upon the initiate in the cadre school. It is not only that his attendance at Party classes is limited to an hour or two a week, or that the authority of these classes is proportionate only to the degree of impact that day-to-day Party pressure has yet been able to make upon his personality; more important, the essence of the cadre schools is applicable to the rank and filer only by analogue. These analogous effects, while of interest in themselves, are intrinsically irrelevant to the study of the moulding of the cadre Communist. Suffice it to say that to the degree that the personal pressure peculiar to the cadre schools can be borne by the rank and filer, classes for the rank and file are so conducted.

THE CADRE SCHOOLS

The tone, the function, the substance of the curriculum, the very methods of teaching, of Communist schools for the cadre are the same in all the Parties of which I have personal experience; and, varying only in their duration and in intensity, the schools are essentially similar at all stages of cadre training: district schools, regional schools, schools for special categories, national schools.[1] Further, my reading concerning Communist schools in other countries, as well as my knowledge of them from discussion with Communists from other Parties, indicates such a similarity throughout the world-wide Communist movement. Nor is this accidental. Quite apart from the international character of the Communist movement with its universal philosophical outlook and the constant and intimate contact between the leaders of the various Parties, the administration, content, and methods of cadre training schools are directly modelled upon the international schools in the Soviet Union, which are the highest schools of the cadres of all the Parties.

But these factors apart, it is not strange that there is a similarity of structure and method throughout the system of Communist training schools. The function of the schools derives from the over-all process of moulding a Communist. The fundamental principles upon which that moulding is based therefore determine the characteristics of the schools. Specifically, these principles are determinant: eradication of every vestige of non-

Communist beliefs and their replacement by the Marxist-Leninist ideology; the psychological transformation of the person into the Communist person; emphasis upon unity of theory and practice; the utilization of pressure, intellectual and psychological, as the decisive tool of training, and, in climax, the inculcation of a final and absolute loyalty to the Party as the necessary and sacred agent and executor of History.

The Party schools are in no way divorced from the whole process of the moulding of the Communist. Rather, they occupy in that process key points, nodes of intense development. Far from being regarded as periods of retirement from "the class struggle," from the constant pressing day-to-day existence of the cadre Communist, they are conceived and organized to carry that urgency of continuous commitment to an even higher level.

SELECTION OF STUDENTS

An index of the high significance of these schools is the way in which students are selected for them. Whereas the details of other aspects of education, agitation and propaganda, as of almost all of the activities of the Party, are in their concrete execution the responsibility of specific commissions and bureaus, the selection of students for training schools is carried out directly by the leading committees of the Party. That is, candidates for a school are nominated by the leading committee of the echelon just below that on which the school is to be conducted, and the ratification or rejection of these nominations is the direct responsibility of the leading committee of the echelon at whose level the school is conducted. Students for an international school are selected by the Political Bureau of the national Parties, and ratified by the international Communist authorities; students for a national school are nominated by District Bureaus and ratified by the Political Bureau of the national Party; students for district schools are nominated by Section Committees and ratified by the responsible District Bureau.

Nor is this, at any echelon, a perfunctory operation. The natural tendency of leading committees, overwhelmed by multifarious responsibilities, to hold back their most capable and effective personnel (in order to avoid the inevitable disruption arising from the removal of a key person for a considerable period of time) is ruthlessly combatted. The phrase is heard again and again in discussion of students for Party schools: "We don't want those who can be spared; we want those who can't be spared." Communists in key Party positions, tested Communist operatives in activity in the external world, those already rising in the cadre: this is the kind of student demanded and secured for Party training schools.[2]

I have emphasized the element of continuity, of the schools as a continuing aspect of the day-to-day processes of the training of the cadre. But at the same time there is a sense in which the schools also represent points of discontinuity, of jumps in the development of the cadreman. Selection for them is always a reward for achievement; successful absorption of their substance and survival of their intensified process of psychological pressure invariably leads to an increase of responsibility, a higher position in the cadre.

FUNCTION OF THE SCHOOLS

The schools are forcing beds. They are consciously organized to achieve conditions in which the student will be artificially tested at a level of Communist consciousness higher than would normally be demanded of him at his present rank. The nearest parallel I know of, outside of the Communist Party, are the special testing courses conducted by organizations like the OSS. There is, however, an important difference. Although I have used the word "artificial" to attempt to indicate an aspect of these Communist schools—there is from the Communist point of view nothing really artificial about them. The content of the activity of the students at cadre training schools is theoretical study, and theoretical study from a Communist point of view is as real and practical an activity as a strike or a demonstration or a political intrigue. The artificiality consists not in the activity, but in the way in which that activity is carried on, so that challenges to the Communist stamina of the student are concentrated in a relatively short period of time. Furthermore, since the absorption of Communist theory is of the greatest importance, the schools thus serve the double function of inculcating theory and testing the Communist personality.

Every circumstance in the organization of the schools is directed towards creating conditions conducive to this latter end. Given the devotion of the students, there is no worry about the absorption of Communist theory. But for students whose life is already highly charged with the tensions ordinary to the Communist who is subject to the moulding process, ways must be found to raise the tensions of the schools to a significantly higher pitch if they are to serve their function.

Physical conditions are designed to isolate the students as much as possible from the world around, even from the normal Party world. Clandestine and conspiratorial arrangements surround the schools, not only when the Party is in one of its periods of illegality or semi-illegality but also when a school could perfectly safely be held quite openly. The director of the school has the fullest Party authority over the students, so that within their artificially created community they live under conditions of constant and direct Party discipline in every aspect of their lives. Every moment of their waking time is under supervision and pressure. Lectures, classes, group discussions, personal study periods, the communal meals, periods of "relaxation," [3] extra-curricular activities such as the writing and editing of "wall newspapers," the presentation of skits, personal conversation and casual observations: everything is an occasion for scrutiny of the words, the attitudes, the scarcely expressed velleities of each student.

The instrument of these pressures is "criticism and self-criticism." This prodding, delving examination and re-examination of intellectual and psychological motive, which by the nature of the case is discontinuous in the day-to-day life of the Communist, becomes in the schools a constant and ever-present phenomenon. From the teachers in formal classes, from the students to each other in study groups, and in the regular formal "self-criticism sessions" under the aegis of the director and other Party leaders, every student is subjected to a constant examination of his consciousness and the degree to which it reflects the Communist ideal. [4]

CURRICULUM

Although every aspect of waking time can provide occasion for this process, the substance of the curriculum serves as the major occasion. A "mistake" in understanding a doctrinal principle, or in analysis of a concrete instance, is never considered corrected by simple intellectual acknowledgment of the "right" answer to the problem. Nor is it even sufficient to trace back to its fundamentals the theoretical "weakness" that brought it about. It is demanded that the reasons for this weakness in turn be examined—emotional failings, the effects of "alien class influences," defects of will, of Communist morality.

The intensity and depth of the curriculum varies with the level and therefore the duration of the school (district schools will last a month to three months; national schools, six months to a year; the international courses from one to three years); but the essential content is universal. Since the purpose of the schools in terms of theoretical indoctrination is to provide a firm foundation of Communist belief, the central themes of the curriculum are the themes I have developed in the discussion of Communist theory in Chapter 4; and to a large degree the division of the curriculum is parallel to the categories there outlined.

One of these categories and one only is not presented formally in the curriculum of any but the very highest schools—that is the philosophical. But this is only an apparent exception. In a very real sense the entire curriculum of all the schools is devoted to indoctrinating the student in the outlook of dialectical materialism. That it is not formally and explicitly taught generally is due to the very characteristics of Communist philosophy and to pedagogical principles based upon those characteristics. Dialectical materialism is conceived as arising so directly out of an understanding of substantive material happenings, that it is believed to be best taught in conjunction with the study of political economy, history, the political theory of Marxism-Leninism, strategy and tactics. Its approaches pervade all other teaching, but a technical study of its principles in the abstract is reserved for those highest levels of understanding where the student will be sure to grasp fully that in reality dialectical materialism does not exist in the abstract.

Otherwise the division of the curriculum follows the essential categories of Communist theory. Even the proportional division of time between the various subjects is approximately uniform in all schools, whether they are longer or shorter. Roughly one-fifth of the available time is generally devoted to Marxist economics (called "political economy" in Communist schools); one-fifth to historical materialism (usually taught in conjunction with a highly stylized Marxist version of the history of "the capitalist era" or of the country in which the school takes place); and the remaining time is divided between political theory (taught as "Marxism-Leninism," often combined with "History of the Communist Party of the Soviet Union"), "strategy and tactics," and a specific discussion of the contemporary Communist line internationally, nationally and in the area in which the Communist work of the student is to be carried out.[5]

(In addition to the central theoretical core of the curriculum, there is always considerable special instruction in practical techniques, varying from the humdrum writing of leaflets and running of mimeograph machines to practical problems of conspiratorial activity, the organization of strikes and demonstrations, and, in some cases, para-military techniques.)

The textbooks are the relevant works of Marx, Engels, Lenin, of Stalin and Mao Tse-tung, and of contemporary Communist leaders internationally and nationally; specific pamphlets and studies on particular questions issued by the Parties (both published works and mimeographed documents for limited inner circulation); and, of course, the latest resolutions and decisions of the Communist leadership.

The mode of teaching is admirably adapted to the ends of the moulding process. While of course the fullest grasp of the subject-matter is demanded of the students, the primary emphasis is not upon their agreement with doctrinal conclusions but upon their complete and integral participation in the "dialectical" way

of arriving at them and upon acceptance of the deepest presuppositions of Marxism-Leninism, an acceptance untinged by
the slightest reservation.[6] Even when, after long and arduous
discussion, a "deviational" concept is cleared up, the fact that
it existed becomes, as I have said, the occasion for fierce and
elaborate analysis of the offender's emotional and personal
"weaknesses" in regular "criticism and self-criticism" sessions
before the entire student body.

Every student in the Party school is put through this process.
And this is planned by the director and the teachers. Most students provide the occasion, either by some "weakness" displayed in class or some hint of a "deviational" attitude exhibited in the course of the life of the school. But when neither
occurs, booby-traps are deliberately planned, designed to catch
the student at what is considered his most vulnerable point, in
order that he may be subjected to concentrated pressure in the
highly intensified form possible only in the semi-artificial conditions of the schools.

The Party school is, in short, an epitome of the process of
moulding Communists. In its function it is in no way discontinuous with that process as it goes on throughout the Communist's
career. The schools a Communist attends do, however, serve to
speed up and sharpen his development—each at key points in
his career. Many fall by the wayside in such schools, fail to
meet the test; and the failure to meet the test (as with the failure
to surmount a crisis) means the interruption, and usually the
end, of their cadre development. But for those who successfully
meet the test, the schools register a distinct advance in their
cadre position. A district school will be the transition point
between secondary responsibilities and absorption into the cadre
of the district leadership; a national school will mark the transi-

tion to top leadership in the district, or in a functional activity of the Party; an international school will bring the Communist who attends it into top leadership of the national Party or into international activity.

The schools compress into a brief time conflicts, tensions, resolutions that would in the ordinary course of events occur only at scattered and irregular intervals. Conflicts, tensions, and their resolutions are the very stuff of the transformation of traditional man into Communist man. The schools in their artificial intensity are forcing beds of the process; but whether applied in these greenhouse conditions or in the open fields of day-to-day Communist activity, the process remains the same. It is devoted to the extirpation of every remnant of philosophical, moral, aesthetic principle or instinct natural to the human being, and the substitution of the principles and instincts of the Communist world-view.

CONCLUSION

The Communist is made, not born. It has been the purpose of this book to show how he is made, and in so doing to illuminate his essence from within, so that he may be conceived in his true being, with an understanding that neither underestimates his strength nor ignores his total enmity, his challenge *à outrance* to our civilization.

The Communist training process exists to create this man. It moulds the person to an ideal image, to the image Communist eschatology dictates. And however each Communist in his different way may fall short of the demands of that ideal, every Communist of the cadre approximates to it. The cadre Communist's understanding of existence is rooted in Marxism-Leninism. His will is hardened to the service of the Communist vision of History and of the Party, its avatar. The whole of his life is Communism; he is held fast to the pole of Communist victory. And by victory he means domination of the world. The Communist is the original totalitarian: his aims are total—
"Morgen die ganze Welt."

His support of humanitarian causes, or of Hitler's savagery;

his bland appeals for peace and disarmament, or his rocket-rattling threats and brutal ultimata; his solicitude for the Alabama Negro and the Bolivian tin-miner, or his ruthless smashing of the Hungarians and the Tibetans: none of these and all of these represent his true being. What he is in his reality no policy, no maneuver, no tactic, no strategy can disclose; he can only be understood if we understand the end to which he is devoted as the compass is drawn to the magnetic pole: the conquest of the world for Communism—with any weapons, so long as they are effective, by any means if they achieve his end . . . and at any cost.

Confronted by this "man of a special mould," tempered in his belief and in his will, infinitely flexible in his methods, the West faces a crisis greater and more demanding than any in its history, greater and more demanding than when in its youth it threw back the armies of Islam. Against this vision, the devotion, the determination of Communist man, there is no recourse in compromise, reasonableness, peaceful co-existence. Only a greater determination can avail, for Communist man poses two stark alternatives for us: victory or defeat.

ACKNOWLEDGMENTS · NOTES · INDEX

ACKNOWLEDGMENTS

For the development and clarification of the concepts that have made the writing of this book possible, I am indebted to so many persons, both through their books and directly, that due and proper acknowledgment is beyond my capability. I should, however, like to say a few words about the books which have aided me, and which may aid the reader, in achieving a deeper understanding of Communism, and to thank organizations and persons who have helped to make possible the materialization of this book.

As far as books are concerned, I have gained greatly from a very large number, both through a suggestion here and there and through confirmation by others of my own experience. The Notes reflect a portion of this debt. I want, however, to single out of the vast literature on Communism those books which have been of the greatest value to me.

On the Communist movement conceived in terms of its strategico-tactical and organizational operations: William R. Kintner, *The Front Is Everywhere;* Nathan Leites, *The Operational Code of the Politburo;* Stefan T. Possony, *A Century of Conflict;* Philip Selznick, *The Organizational Weapon.*

For a general over-all view of the Communist movement as a historical and social phenomenon: Jules Monnerot, *The Sociology and Psychology of Communism;* A. Rossi's three volumes on the Communist Party of France (*Physiologie du Parti Communiste Français, Les Communistes Français pendant la Drôle de Guerre;*

La Politique de la Résistance, 1940-1944), the first of which has been translated by Willmoore Kendall as *A Communist Party in Action.*

On the specific aspect with which this book is concerned, the subjective side—the Communist movement seen in its ethos, pictured in terms of the personality, consciousness, and outlook which guide it and drive it forward—the best books I know are three novels and an autobiography: Arthur Koestler, *Darkness at Noon;* Victor Serge, *The Case of Comrade Tulayev;* Manès Sperber, *The Burned Bramble;* and Whittaker Chambers, *Witness.*

My indebtedness directly to persons is so great and at the same time so kaleidoscopic that I find myself completely unable to specify. Besides, the final form of what I have written is my own responsibility, and no one else, however helpful he has been in stimulating and crystallizing what is here presented, should even by the widest implication bear the burden of responsibility for it. Suffice it to say that I am indebted to very many: friends; scholars in politics, history, philosophy, theology; former Communists; casual questioners, accidentally met or from the floor of meetings.

I can be more precise in my thanks to those who have in various ways given encouragement and assistance in moving this book from a concept to a reality: James Burnham, Whittaker Chambers, Moshe Decter, Nathan Glazer, Herbert E. Krugman, Ithiel De Sola Pool, Ralph de Toledano, Sylvia Weyl, Karl A. Wittfogel.

Further in this regard, I want to express my appreciation for the financial assistance given to this study in its early stages by The RAND Corporation.

And to the Fund for the Republic I express my appreciation for their financial assistance during the completion of the book. In particular, I want to thank Clinton Rossiter, the General Editor of this Fund for the Republic series on Communism in American Life, whose courtesy, forbearance, and friendliness have helped me in a hundred ways.

I wish to express my gratitude to Anna Walters, who typed the manuscript with scrupulous accuracy.

Finally and first, I cannot measure how much is owed to my wife, Elsie Bown Meyer—without whom, no book.

NOTES

CHAPTER TWO: THE MOULD

1. G. Dimitroff, *The United Front Against Fascism and War* (New York, Workers Library Publishers, 1935), p. 46.

2. An interesting confirmation of my own observation of this use of "our people" is contained in the *Report of the Royal Commission* (Ottawa, Edmond Cloutier, 1946), investigating Soviet espionage following upon the disclosures made by Igor Gouzenko, cipher clerk in the Soviet Embassy in Canada: "The attitude of members of the Soviet Embassy staff toward 'developed' members of the Canadian Communist Party is well summed up in the Russian word 'NASH,' occasionally used as a sentence by itself with reference to members of that Party in Colonel Zabotin's notebooks. 'NASH,' literally translated, means 'OURS' or 'HE IS OURS' " (p. 29).

3. Cf.: "From the highest to the lowest the select cadres are ever more closely modelled upon this [Stalinist] prototype. It is the emergence of a new social type. . . . They are *party products. . . .*" (Emphasis in original.) Jules Monnerot, *Sociology and Psychology of Communism* (Boston, The Beacon Press, 1953), p. 96.

Also: ". . . il [the Party] leur donne une doctrine, il entretient chez eux une mystique, il leur assigne des tâches adéquates, aptes à les former et à les sélectionner. *L'action multiple du parti est, à cet effet, un creuset dont la haute témperature brûle ou trempe ceux qui y passent."* (My emphasis.) A. Rossi, *Physiologie du Parti Communiste Français* (Paris, Éditions Self, 1948), p. 275.

4. I am, of course, aware of the fact that there is a strong body of opinion, represented by such studies as Almond *et al., The Appeals of Communism* (Princeton, N. J., Princeton University Press, 1954), which maintains that certain specific psychological structures are typical of those who are drawn to Communism—at least when immediate personal economic interests are not present. My differences with this position are developed more fully in the subsequent chapter on the process of recruiting. But for the point at issue here, it is not important whether a few or many types make up the raw material upon which the Communist moulding process operates. The process remains essentially the same—that of imposing an ideal type upon an "alien personality"—whether the varieties of that personality are many or few.

5. Cf.: "In Communist jargon to be a 'cadre' meant to be someone trained and ready to do anything, anywhere for communism. The task of the Party was and is to produce 'men of a special mold,' as Stalin called them in his speech at Lenin's funeral. They must, like Stalin, be 'men of steel,' hard, inflexible, rapier edged. To be a 'steel-hardened cadre' became the aim of every good Party member." Douglas Hyde, *I Believed* (New York, G. P. Putnam's Sons, 1950), p. 92.

Also: "Here we again discover a basic law of operation of Communist parties: in order to direct the movement of the masses a party must first create the strong skeleton of a body which will take on flesh according to circumstances. When circumstances become critical, the body may be reduced to the skeleton, but the skeleton will not disintegrate." Jean-Marie Domenach writing on the French Party in Mario Einaudi, Jean-Marie Domenach, and Aldo Garosci, *Communism in Western Europe* (Ithaca, Cornell University Press, 1951), p. 71.

Also: ". . . le parti ne pourrait pas exister sans des cadres permanents et solides, sans une certain 'continuité' qui survive aux changements d'hommes et de tactique. Il doit pouvoir compter sur la fidélité . . . surtout de ses militants 'responsables.' Le parti vaut finalement ce que valent ces derniers. D'où l'extrême importance qu'a pour lui une bonne 'politique des cadres.' " A. Rossi, *Physiologie du Parti Communiste Français,* p. 337.

Also: ". . . the communist movement itself is composed of layers of adherents who, relative to a controlling group, function as masses. First there is the hard core of self-conscious agents within the party who are fully aware of the central role of power in bolshevism. Their commitment is so deep that it need not be shored up by hatreds, by symbols, or by other forms of mass persuasion. These are the steeled cadres upon whom the continuity and the basic power of the party rest. They constitute the fundamental support of the decisionmaking group because they identify with the power aims of the movement and are ready to defend twists in the party line before the general membership. This group may constitute no more than one-tenth of a large party such as the French Communist Party; among American party members the proportion is probably higher." Philip Selznick, *The Organizational Weapon* (New York, McGraw-Hill Book Co., 1952), pp. 83-84.

6. It is true that the word "cadre" is sometimes used in the Parties in other senses, closer to the original military derivation, as well as in the fundamental Communist sense discussed here. Thus it is possible to speak of "the cadres of the trade-union movement" or "the Party cadre in the Peace Movement." For example, in *A Documentary History of Chinese Communism* by Conrad Brandt, Benjamin Schwartz and John K. Fairbank (Cambridge, Harvard University Press, 1952), one finds the two usages side by side.

Cf., on the one hand, Mao Tse-tung: "The audience for literature and art is made up of the workers, peasants, soldiers, and their cadres . . ." (p. 410), that is, in the secondary usage; while a few pages before in the "Central Committee Decision on Methods of Leadership, of July 1, 1943," the word is used in the other, the primary sense, the sense of the cadre of the Party: ". . . standards for this leading core should be the four criteria for cadres proposed by Dimitrov" (p. 375).

7. Joseph Stalin, *Foundations of Leninism* (New York, International Publishers, 1939), p. 116.

8. Cf.: "To me, small fry among such big fish, there was some satisfaction in watching these men being roundly abused for

falling short of their Party duty. If a non-Communist labor leader ever said one-tenth to these men of what Pollitt and Burns used to say, they would bring their unions out in a raging strike. But they sit still, humbly and patiently, when a member of the Party's Executive charges them with negligence. Men like Arthur Horner, Jim Gardener, Abe Moffatt, John Horner [top leaders of the British trade-union movement], may eat fire in public, but the dish is humble pie at NIPC meetings [National Industrial Policy Committee of the Central Committee of the Communist Party of Great Britain]." Bob Darke, *Cockney Communist* (New York, The John Day Co., 1953), p. 76. The whole of this book, as a matter of fact, is, albeit unconsciously, a beautiful picture of the position of a Communist trade-union leader, with considerable stature in his union and no mean position in the official Party, who is nevertheless totally outside of the cadre.

Cf. also Manès Sperber, *The Burned Bramble* (New York, Doubleday & Co., 1951), for the relations between Party cadre and formal Party leaders, even those with great mass following, in Yugoslavia and Central Europe before World War II.

9. Cf.: "We are believers. Not as you are. We do not believe either in God or in men. We manufacture gods and we transform men. We believe in Order. We will create a universe in our image, without weaknesses, a universe in which man, rid of the old rags of Christianity, will attain his cosmic grandeur, in the supreme culmination of the species. We are not fighting for a regime, or for power, or for riches. *We are the instruments of Fate.*" (Emphasis mine.) The statement of a young Soviet official quoted by Arthur Koestler, *The Invisible Writing* (New York, The Macmillan Co., 1954), pp. 155-156, from J. L. Bruckberger, *One Sky to Share* (New York, P. J. Kenedy & Sons, 1952).

10. "The Lenin Heritage," in Joseph Stalin, *Lenin,* Little Lenin Library (New York, International Publishers, 1934), Vol. 16, p. 15.

11. Dimitroff, *The United Front,* p. 47.

12. *History of the Communist Party of the Soviet Union (Bolsheviks)* (New York, International Publishers, 1939), pp. 353-356.

13. Dimitroff, *The United Front,* pp. 48-49.

14. *Ibid.,* p. 47.

15. *Ibid.,* p. 47.

16. See Arthur Koestler, *Darkness at Noon,* and a most revealing passage concerning the confession of Mrachkovsky, a veteran of the Revolution and the Civil War, in W. G. Krivitsky, *In Stalin's Secret Service* (New York, Harper & Brothers, 1939), pp. 198-203.

17. Cf.: "A professional revolutionist is ready to go whenever and wherever the Party sends him. Today he may be working in a mine, organizing the Party, the trade unions, leading struggles; tomorrow, if the Party so decides, he may be in a steel mill; the day after tomorrow, he may be a leader and organizer of the unemployed." J. Peters, *The Communist Party—A Manual on Organization* (Workers Library Publishers, July, 1935), reprinted in *Hearings,* Appendix, Part I, U.S. House Special Committee on Un-American Activities, 76th Cong., 1st sess., Washington, 1940, p. 734.

Also: "Interchangeability of units and personnel is the foremost advantage gained . . . a Kremlin trouble shooter can direct a Communist party anywhere in the world with but the briefest orientation.

"The *Report* of the House Committee on Foreign Affairs, *Five Hundred Leading Communists,* commented on the ease with which the Communist high command shifts its personnel from one detachment of the party military machine to another: 'Joanny Berlioz of the French Communist Party . . . shifted to Algerian work when deported to Algiers, and back to the French Party, Chou En-lai of China . . . worked both in the French and Chinese Parties, and Stefan Jedrychowski of Poland . . . apparently had no difficulty in assuming a prominent role in Poland and Lithuania from time to time.' Such shifts are possible only because the paramilitary Communist party follows a standard organizational pattern in every country of the world." William R. Kintner, *The Front Is Everywhere* (Norman, Oklahoma: University of Oklahoma Press, 1950), p. 51.

18. Lenin, *"Left Wing" Communism, An Infantile Disorder* (London, The Communist Party of Great Britain, 1928), p. 12.

19. Dimitroff, *The United Front,* p. 47.

20. *History of the C.P.S.U.(B.),* pp. 362-363.

21. Cf.: ". . . bolshevik cadres cannot be created simply through indoctrination; they are trained and tested *in* the struggle for

power. A leadership party must have something to lead, or some group for whose control a struggle can be carried on." Philip Selznick, *The Organizational Weapon*, p. 19.

22. For a profound discussion of one type of such crisis, see Whittaker Chambers, *Witness* (New York, Random House, 1952), pp. 12-17. This problem is analyzed in the chapter on the cadre.

23. Bertolt Brecht, "Die Massnahme," *Gesammelte Werke*, II; translation from Ruth Fischer's *Stalin and German Communism* (Cambridge, Harvard University Press, 1948), p. 620. The play "Die Massnahme" as a whole is a remarkable poetical presentation of the ideal type of the Communist.

24. Dimitroff, *The United Front*, pp. 47-48.

25. Cf.: "Bolshevism . . . can be considered as one of the few successful movements of pure will in history. . . ." Daniel Bell, "Bolshevik Man, His Motivations," *Commentary*, February, 1955, p. 183.

CHAPTER THREE: THE MECHANISM OF PRESSURE: THE PARTY

1. Cf.: "Pour le parti communiste . . . le problème des cadres est essentiel. Aucun autre parti ne se l'est posé jusqu'à présent avec autant d'intensité et de méthode. Il l'envisage comme un problème *politique,* dont doivent continuer à s'occuper les dirigeants du parti, même lorsqu'ils se font aider, dans la bonne gestion des cadres, par des 'responsables' qui en sont spécialement chargés. Ainsi on peut lire, dans un article consacré au travail des cadres, des critiques adressées au secrétaire d'une grande région:

'Dans une grande région, on a le regret d'entendre le sécretaire tenir le langage suivant: "Depuis que j'ai mis un responsable aux cadres, moi, je ne veux plus savoir qui sont les camarades qui font le travail; quand j'ai besoin d'un homme ou d'une femme, je le demande au responsable des cadres." Est-il possible de croire que, parce qu'on a désigné un responsable au travail des cadres—ce qui est actuellement indispensable,—on a fait sa tâche dans le domaine des cadres? Non, c'est impossible: le problème des cadres est infiniment plus large. *C'est le problème de tout le parti!* "

A. Rossi, *Physiologie du Parti Communiste Français,* p. 289; emphasis in original.

2. The universal prevalence of the Communist emphasis upon absolute precision of concept and formulation and absolute rejection of any deviation, however infinitesimal, has been widely remarked. I think Czeslaw Milosz has, however, grasped the quality of the phenomenon most closely: "Only the bourgeois persists in thinking that nothing results from these nuances of thought. The Party knows that much can come of them: there was a time when the Revolution was merely a nuance in the thinking of a little group of theoreticians led by Lenin, quarreling around a café table in Switzerland. . . . The difference of a tiny fraction in the premises yields dizzying differences after the calculation is completed. A deviation from the line in the evaluation of some work of art may become the leaven of a political upheaval." *The Captive Mind* (New York, Alfred A. Knopf, 1953), pp. 213-214.

"Is 'Bolshevik' character the same as it was fifty years ago? In important respects yes. . . . Prerevolutionary behavior toward rival political organizations once displayed itself in small cafés and drafty meeting halls; now its scene is the great assembly halls of world politics: the same behavior repeats itself. The preoccupation with procedural issues—*arising from the belief that a small point will 'inevitably' grow into a big one and must not be conceded*—which was displayed by Lenin on the constitution of the editorial board of *Iskra* in 1900 (when he was 'co-existing' with rival Social Democrats), is duplicated in intra-party disputes in 1921, and again at international negotiations at Yalta, San Francisco, and the conference of foreign ministers in 1945." Daniel Bell, "Bolshevik Man, His Motivations," *Commentary,* February, 1955, p. 181; my emphasis.

3. *Cahiers du Communisme,* January, 1949, p. 96.

4. *The Communist,* February, 1932, p. 123.

5. Lenin, *Selected Works* (New York, International Publishers), Vol. 3, pp. 110-111.

6. This stance of personal responsibility as regent for the Party involves the concept of the Party as a totally autonomous and hostile society within society and over against it. Therefore, the Party and "its people" must possess a sense of total responsibility which no member of an articulated society, not even the highest or most powerful, can have.

Cf. Rossi: "Le parti, en outre, est comme un État dans l'État, le 'deuxième pouvoir' dont on participe. Là où le mouvement communiste est important, ses dirigeants disposent souvent d'un pouvoir plus grand que les ministres ou les préfets, traitent avec eux—directement ou non—de puissance à puissance, mettent en branle les masses, interviennent à chaque instant dans la vie du pays, exercent sur elle une pression efficace. On est une force avec laquelle il faut compter. Chaque 'responsable' communiste est, à son échelon, un chef, qui a droit 'de vie et de mort' sur d'autres hommes, que ce soient les deux camarades de son groupe ou les milliers de militants d'une région." *Physiologie du Parti Communiste Français*, p. 341.

7. This aspect of the Communist *Weltanschauung* is depicted with great intensity, particularly as it affects the creative artist in Communist countries, by Czeslaw Milosz, *The Captive Mind.* See especially Chapter VIII, "Man, this Enemy." ". . . the Party," he writes, "fights any tendency to delve into the depths of a human being, especially in literature and art. Whoever reflects on 'man' in general, on his inner needs and longings, is accused of bourgeois sentimentality. . . . *What is not expressed does not exist.* Therefore if one forbids men to explore the depths of human nature, one destroys in them the urge to make such explorations; and the depths in themselves slowly become unreal" (p. 215; emphasis in original).

Cf. also Koestler recounting the well-known Malraux anecdote: "For the pressure of that [Communist] environment seems almost irresistible—slow and steady like soil erosion, or the action of the tides. . . . It cuts man off from his metaphysical roots, from religious experience, from the 'oceanic feeling' in all its forms. Cosmic awareness is replaced by social vigilance, perception of the absolute by brain-acrobatics. The result is a gradual dehydration of the soul, a spiritual dearth more frightening than the famine. . . . At a Writers' Congress in Moscow, after listening to countless speeches promising universal happiness in a brave new world, André Malraux asked suddenly: 'And what about the child run over by a tram car?' There was a pained silence; then somebody said, amidst general approbation: 'In a perfect, planned socialist transport system there will be no accidents.'" (*The Invisible Writing*, pp. 157-158.)

8. Cf.: "Harry Pollitt it was, I think who said, 'Every Communist in a capitalist society is a capitalist at heart.' This wasn't a

matter of benevolent tolerance, it was a warning to all comrades to beware of the non-Communist fifth column within themselves. When a Communist is disturbed by the voice of his conscience he remembers the words of Pollitt and drowns it." Bob Darke, *Cockney Communist,* p. 17.

9. It is this concept which is reflected rather picturesquely by Mao Tse-tung in a discussion of the Cheng Feng movement (a bolshevization campaign of the Communist Party of China in the early forties): "If the reasoning is good, if it is to the point, it can be effective. The first method in reasoning is to give the patients a powerful stimulus, yell at them 'you're sick!' so the patients will have a fright and break out in an over-all sweat; then, they can be carefully treated." Brandt, Schwartz and Fairbank, *A Documentary History of Chinese Communism,* p. 396.

10. With one great exception, these methods have always been confined to Party members, even in the Soviet Union and in the countries of Eastern Europe where the Communist Parties are in power. That exception has been in the practice of the Communist Party of China in recent years. That Party has extended the methods, with appropriate variations, beyond the Party membership. This rather remarkable innovation in Communist practice has, to my knowledge, been previously remarked *for what it is* only by Douglas Hyde: "Communist indoctrination classes, during the course of which a man's whole approach to life is turned upside down and the way prepared for the acceptance of a new philosophy, are almost as old as the Communist party itself. But they were always confined to party members and sympathizers. That is broadly true even of Russia. But in China the Communists . . . have undertaken the enormous task of trying to put the whole of their vast population through a process of indoctrination." Douglas Hyde, "Mao: New Prophet of World Communism," *America,* March 19, 1955, pp. 641-642. This innovation is, of course, the process translated by Edward Hunter as "brainwashing," and described first by him in *Brainwashing in Red China* (New York, Vanguard Press, 1951).

11. The extreme importance of this factor as an element in the pressure the Party exerts on the individual is hard to appreciate unless it has been experienced; and very few books on Communism concern themselves with the content of day-to-day

activity on any level. Two books, however, both by rank and filers, do give a vivid impression of this aspect of the life of a Communist: Angela Calomiris, *Red Masquerade* (Philadelphia, J. B. Lippincott Co., 1950) and Bob Darke, *Cockney Communist*. In the latter see particularly Chapter 7, pp. 125-145. There is also, from an earlier period, a good description of this aspect of the rank and filer's life in Benjamin Gitlow, *I Confess* (New York, E. P. Dutton & Co., 1940), pp. 288 ff. And for the Communist Party of the Soviet Union, see Merle Fainsod: "The life of the Party member is ordinarily a busy and demanding one. As a member of an élite group, he is privileged, but he is also duty-bound. At work he is expected to set an example of devotion; his so-called leisure hours are filled with extra-curricular Party duties and assignments. A recent Soviet *émigré* who had formerly been a Party member said: 'You have to attend meetings, pay dues, go to the Party School, study the short course of the history of the Party, study the works of Marx, Lenin, and Stalin, read the Party newspapers, explain the decisions of the Party to non-Party people, take part in putting up wall newspapers, at the time of election you have to be an agitator. . . .'" *How Russia Is Ruled* (Cambridge, Harvard University Press, 1953), p. 199.

12. Cf. Rossi: "Le parti tend à créer chez ses membres un *automatisme* de réactions qui sont pour lui une indispensable garantie d'homogénéité et de cohésion. Il ne s'agit point d'un automatisme banal, car le parti ne peut et ne veut pas détruire la volonté d'action, ni l'intelligence qui la guide et l'anime. Mais intelligence et conscience ne sont valables qu'à un certain degré: il en faut juste autant que l'exigent, dans chaque situation, les buts que le parti se propose. C'est un automatisme qui doit gagner les centres supérieurs de l'homme, s'adapter à leur fonctionnement pour mieux les subordonner, en employant les ressources d'une psychologie et d'une pédagogie averties pour obtenir un parfait *dressage* avec un maximum de rendement." *Physiologie du Parti Communiste Français*, pp. 298-299; emphasis in original.

13. This lack of shame before the Party, this complete acceptance of its dictates, no matter how they might seem to dishonor the person, has its classic expression for the Russian Communist leader in Arthur Koestler's *Darkness at Noon* (London,

Jonathan Cape, 1944). See the prison-tapped debate between the Czarist officer and Rubashov:

"Smiling to himself, he [Rubashov] tapped with his pince-nez:

"I AM CAPITULATING.

"He waited curiously for the effect.

"For a long while nothing came; No. 402 was silenced. His answer came a whole minute later:

"I'D RATHER HANG . . .

"Rubashov smiled. He tapped:

"EACH ACCORDING TO HIS KIND.

"He had expected an outbreak of anger from No. 402. Instead, the tapping sign sounded subdued, as it were, resigned:

"I WAS INCLINED TO CONSIDER YOU AN EXCEPTION. HAVE YOU NO SPARK OF HONOUR LEFT?

"Rubashov lay on his back, his pince-nez in his hand. He felt contented and peaceful. He tapped:

"OUR IDEAS OF HONOUR DIFFER.

"No. 402 tapped quickly and precisely:

"HONOUR IS TO LIVE AND DIE FOR ONE'S BELIEF.

"Rubashov answered just as quickly:

"HONOUR IS TO BE USEFUL WITHOUT VANITY.

"No. 402 answered this time louder and more sharply:

"HONOUR IS DECENCY—NOT USEFULNESS.

"WHAT IS DECENCY? asked Rubashov, comfortably spacing the letters. The more calmly he tapped, the more furious became the knocking in the wall.

"SOMETHING YOUR KIND WILL NEVER UNDERSTAND, answered No. 402 to Rubashov's question. Rubashov shrugged his shoulders:

"WE HAVE REPLACED DECENCY BY REASON, he tapped back.

"No. 402 did not answer any more." (Pp. 168-169.)

If the peculiar lack of shame before the Party in Rubashov may be thought to be a function of high leadership in a Communist country, Richard Wright has given its parallel in a disciplinary trial of the Communist Party of the United States, in the Negro South Side of Chicago:

"The trial began in a quiet, informal manner. The comrades acted like a group of neighbours sitting in judgment upon one of their kind who had stolen a chicken. Anybody could ask and get the floor. There was absolute freedom of speech. Yet the meeting had an amazingly formal structure of its own, a structure that went as deep as the desire of men to live together.

"A member of the Central Committee of the Communist Party rose and gave a description of the world situation. He spoke without emotion and piled up hard facts. He painted a horrible but masterful picture of Fascism's aggression in Germany, Italy, and Japan. . . .

"The next speaker discussed the role of the Soviet Union as the world's lone workers' state—how the Soviet Union was hemmed in by enemies, how the Soviet Union was trying to industrialize itself, what sacrifices it was making to help workers of the world to steer a path toward peace through the idea of collective security. . . .

"Finally a speaker came forward and spoke of Chicago's South Side, its Negro population, their suffering and handicaps, linking all that also to the world struggle. Then still another speaker followed and described the tasks of the Communist Party of the South Side. At last, the world, the national, and the local pictures had been fused into one overwhelming drama of moral struggle in which everybody in the hall was participating. This presentation had lasted for more than three hours, but it had enthroned a new sense of reality in the hearts of those present, a sense of man on earth. With the exception of the church and its myths and legends, there is no agency in the world so capable of making men feel the earth and the people upon it as the Communist Party.

"Toward evening the direct charges against Ross were made, not by the leaders of the Party, but by Ross's friends, those who knew him best! It was crushing. Ross wilted. His emotions could not withstand the weight of the moral pressure. No one was terrorized into giving information against him. They gave it willingly, citing dates, conversations, scenes. The black mass of Ross's wrongdoing emerged slowly and irrefutably.

"The moment came for Ross to defend himself. I had been told that he had arranged for friends to testify on his behalf, but he called upon no one. He stood, trembling; he tried to talk and his words would not come. The hall was as still as death. Guilt was written in every pore of his black skin. His hands shook. He held on to the edge of the table to keep on his feet.

His personality, his sense of himself, had been obliterated. Yet he could not have been so humbled unless he had shared and accepted the vision that had crushed him, the common vision that bound us all together.

" 'Comrades,' he said in a low, charged voice, 'I'm guilty of all the charges, all of them.'

"His voice broke in a sob. No one prodded him. No one tortured him. No one threatened him. He was free to go out of the hall and never see another Communist. But he did not want to. He could not. . . .

"It was not a fear of the Communist Party that had made him confess, but a fear of the punishment that he would exact of himself that made him tell of his wrongdoings. The Communists had talked to him until they had given him new eyes with which to see his own crime. And then they sat back and listened to him tell how he had erred. He was one with all the members there, regardless of race or colour; his heart was theirs and their hearts were his; and when a man reaches that state of kinship with others, that degree of oneness, or when a trial has made him kin, after he has been sundered from them by wrongdoing, then he must rise and say, out of a sense of the deepest morality in the world: 'I'm guilty. Forgive me!' " *The God That Failed*, ed., Richard Crossman (New York, Harper & Bros., 1949), pp. 154-157.

CHAPTER FOUR: PHILOSOPHICAL

PRESSURE: MARXISM-LENINISM

1. Cf. Raymond A. Bauer, *The New Man in Soviet Psychology* (Cambridge, Harvard University Press, 1952): "The basic principle of modern Soviet didactics is the principle of conscious understanding" (p. 163). "The Bolshevik controls man by training his motives and shaping his ideology; he then expects an individual consciously, and unfailingly, to carry out the task assigned to him. . . . The Bolshevik insists on man's responsibility for his behavior and on his ability to make his own destiny. He follows the Party line because the Party is 'right' and because he presumably understands why it is right . . ." (pp. 177-178).

2. ". . . *basically, the ideology* [of the Soviet rulers], *however altered and shaped, remains the framework within which decisions are made.* While national interests are strong, their implementation is predicated upon Marxist methodology. In fact it is difficult to imagine any other philosophical concept commanding the allegiance of the men in the Kremlin. Nurtured on Marxism, they have, since Lenin, been exposed to no other system or idea." Robert Paul Browder, "The Two Faces of Soviet Foreign Policy," *Colorado Quarterly*, Winter, 1955, p. 260; my emphasis.

"The tremendous militancy of the Soviet government—'dynamism' is the polite new term—*stems* not from any inherent qualities of the Russian nation but *from the* warlike and messianic *ideology of its Communist rulers.*" David J. Dallin, *The New Soviet Empire* (London, Hollis & Carter, 1951), p. 72; my emphasis.

"Cette même constation [as for members of the Communist Party of France] vaut pour les membres du parti bolchevik, et celui qui la néglige est condamné à ne rien comprendre de la situation actuelle de l'U.R.S.S." A. Rossi, *Physiologie du Parti Communiste Français*, p. 320, ftn. 2.

3. "The party could not exist without the ideology providing its doctrinal legitimacy. Ideology may be manipulated to suit policy, but it is still there, not merely reflecting the needs of the rulers but shaping their mentalities as well. Doctrinal rationalization has not ended with Lenin, nor has falsification ended with Stalin. . . . The history of Soviet thought can be regarded as a struggle of doctrine with reality, or as a process of adjustment to intractable reality. When the latter is finally accepted, the doctrinal formula of acceptance is referred to as 'the creative development of Marxism.'" Leopold Labedz, "Ideology: The Fourth Stage," *Problems of Communism*, Nov.-Dec., 1959, p. 3.

4. "Communism in action is today a very intricate religion of power. The ideology of Communism has been neither abandoned nor pushed aside in the expansionist drive of Soviet Russia. It has become an integral part of the interpretation of political power by the masters of world Communism. Collectivization, political terror, industrial planning, and mass education and indoctrination are not separate items of a political program, either as relics of earlier idealism or as results of

today's corruption, but they all fit together into the composite picture of the Communist understanding of political power." Adam B. Ulam, *Titoism and the Cominform* (Cambridge, Harvard University Press, 1952), p. 230.

5. "Communism is thus a *Weltanschauung* based upon a closely articulated body of doctrine—philosophic, economic, political and social—which claims alone to provide the scientific explanation of the world. It has to be studied as a whole, and it is impermissible to abstract from it certain elements which may happen to interest us and to ignore the others. It is impossible to understand communist activity without a knowledge of the system upon which it rests. Every Communist who holds any important position has been well instructed in it so that he knows just where he stands, and has an answer to everything, which is far from being the case with the majority of his opponents; and to discuss any problem with an intelligent and politically developed Communist is to become aware that he is living in a different climate of opinion from our own and that his values are not ours." R. N. Carew Hunt, *The Theory and Practice of Communism* (New York, The Macmillan Company, 1954), p. 7.

6. Cf.: "For the communist believer thinks his doctrine, as a system of dogmas, is rational; and the rational, in his opinion, is an anticipation of the real. Therefore the irrational element in the world must be progressively reduced *until the rational and the real are completely and finally equated.*" Jules Monnerot, *Sociology and Psychology of Communism*, p. 185; emphasis in original.

7. Lenin, *Materialism and Empirio-Criticism,* in *Selected Works* (New York, International Publishers, 1943), Vol. XI, p. 205.

8. Karl Marx, Second Thesis on Feuerbach, *The German Ideology* (New York, International Publishers, 1939), p. 197.

9. Cf. Mao Tse-tung: "All key Party workers on the various levels throughout the land should all understand that the close union of theory and practice is one of the salient features by which our Communists are distinguished from all other political parties." "On Coalition Government, April 24, 1945," in Conrad Brandt, Benjamin Schwartz, and John K. Fairbank, *A Documentary History of Chinese Communism*, p. 316. Also: "As the study of theory is normally uncongenial to our

national temperament, it is commonly argued that the present Russian rulers are hard-headed realists who believe in nothing, that they are simply engaged upon 'power politics' and that the Communist Parties which they direct act likewise. In this event we need only be concerned with their practice, and may regard their theories as no more than *ex post facto* rationalisations. Yet there is no doubt that Communists do believe that they are applying to political situations a theory which they fervently accept and which they hold to be scientific. . . . Communists never forget their own theoretical principles. . . . [This] reflects . . . the belief that Marxism is a science, and that communist strategy and tactics derive from it by strictly logical deduction." R. N. Carew Hunt, *The Theory and Practice of Communism*, p. v.

10. Lenin, "The Tasks of the Youth Leagues," in *Selected Works* (New York, International Publishers, 1943), Vol. IX, pp. 475-478.

11. "What vileness would you not commit to
     exterminate vileness?
Could you change the world, for what
     would you be too good?
Who are you?
Sink into the mud,
     embrace the butcher, but
     change the world: it needs it."

Song of the Controlchorus from Bertolt Brecht's "Die Mass-nahme," translation from Ruth Fischer's *Stalin and German Communism* (Cambridge, Harvard University Press, 1948), p. 622.

"The question, Comrade, shows that you are thinking in mecha-nistic, not in dialectical, terms. What is the difference between a gun in the hands of a policeman and a gun in the hands of a member of the revolutionary working class? The difference be-tween a gun in the hands of a policeman and in the hands of a member of the revolutionary working class is that the policeman is a lackey of the ruling class and his gun an instrument of op-pression, whereas the same gun in the hands of a member of the revolutionary working class is an instrument of the libera-tion of the oppressed masses." Arthur Koestler in *The God That Failed*, p. 47.

"The choice of weapons is governed exclusively by their effectiveness." Jules Monnerot, *Sociology and Psychology of Communism,* p. 256.

12. Engels, *Anti-Dühring* (New York, International Publishers, n.d.), pp. 130-131.

13. This phrase, constantly heard in the Parties, is a rather less subtle variation of the classic Marxist doctrine. That doctrine, however, is essentially expressed by it. That is, there are no events which are not subject to the laws of historical materialism. There are, in Engels' words, "things and events whose inner connection is so remote or so impossible to prove that we regard it as absent and can neglect it" (No. 213, Letter to Bloch, *Correspondence, 1846-1895, of Karl Marx and Friedrich Engels, A Selection* [New York, International Publishers, 1935], p. 475); or, as Marx says, such "accidents" as "fall naturally into the general course of development and are compensated for, again, by other accidents" (No. 153, Letter to Kugelmann, *ibid.,* p. 311). But, however things may appear on the surface, fundamentally there is no place in Marxist-Leninist theory for the event ungoverned by the laws of historical materialism. The *locus classicus* on the question is Engels' discussion in *Ludwig Feuerbach* (New York, International Publishers, 1935), which concludes: "Historical events . . . appear on the whole to be . . . governed by chance. But where on the surface accident holds sway, there actually it is always governed by inner, hidden laws, and it is only a matter of discovering these laws" (p. 58).

14. Karl Marx, *The Critique of Political Economy* (Chicago, Charles H. Kerr & Co., 1904), p. 11.

15. *Ibid.,* p. 12.

16. Kautsky, quoted by Lenin as a central and integral part of his argument in *What Is To Be Done?* (*Selected Works,* Vol. II, pp. 61-62).

17. Lenin, *What Is To Be Done?,* in *Selected Works,* Vol. II, p. 47.

18. *History of the Communist Party of the Soviet Union (Bolsheviks)* (New York, International Publishers, 1939), p. 353.

19. Stalin, *Foundations of Leninism,* p. 53.

20. The Communist criticism of Stalin after his death was directed not against the use of force as force, but against capricious

acts of force—acts harmful to the Party not because they were terroristic, but because they were wrongly directed.

21. Stalin, *Foundations of Leninism,* p. 101.

22. "The Soviet system by its very nature attempts to secure the universality of its absolutes, as stipulated by Soviet ideology. Any given policy expresses to some degree this underlying motivation. The larger the obstacle, apparent or real, facing such universalization, the less emphasis is put on universalization itself and the more [on the] flexible components of policy designed to cope with and eventually disintegrate the obstacles. Once this objective is accomplished, the true goal of policy resumes its full role. The aim of Soviet ideology—domination of the world—does not change; strategy, operational direction, tactics, and propaganda do." Jan F. Triska, "A Model for Study of Soviet Foreign Policy," *American Political Science Review,* March, 1958, pp. 70-71.

23. Cf.: "It is the vision of man's liberated mind, by the sole force of its rational intelligence, redirecting man's destiny and re-organizing man's life and the world." Whittaker Chambers, *Witness,* p. 9.

CHAPTER FIVE: PSYCHOLOGICAL PRESSURE

1. "The Party line must be rationally calculated and must be distinguished from 'moods' both within the Party and without, that might affect it. . . . 'Replacing objective analysis by "feelings" '—to *any* extent—threatens catastrophe. . . . A Bolshevik must have perfect control over his feelings. All his political activity is 'a most coldblooded . . . war.' Any imperfection in the Bolshevik's control over his feelings will cause him to become dominated by them. This will result in catastrophe. . . . These precepts hold true even when the feelings are in themselves laudable: a 'revolutionary out of sentiment' is not a 'real revolutionary.' " Nathan Leites, *The Operational Code of the Politburo* (New York, McGraw-Hill Book Co., 1951), p. 20; emphasis in original.

2. Marx and Engels, *The German Ideology,* p. 7.

3. *Ibid.,* p. 75.

4. "The interests of the Party above all—this is the highest prin-

ciple. . . . The Party member should see that he has only the Party and Party interests in mind and no individual purpose. He should see that his own individual interests are identical with Party interests to the extent that they are fused. When contradictions arise between the interests of the Party and the individual we can, without the slightest hesitation or feeling of compulsion, submit to Party interests and sacrifice the individual." Liu Shao-ch'i, *The Training of the Communist Party Member,* as quoted in Robert C. North, *Moscow and Chinese Communists* (Stanford, California, Stanford University Press, 1953), p. 199.

5. "The constant theme of bourgeois psychology is the problem of inner personality conflicts; the eternal struggle of two entities —the human and the animal; the conscious and the unconscious; the rational and the instinctual; the social and the biological, and so on, which lead to the notorious split personality. The tenacity with which these theories persist can be largely attributed to their usefulness to the scientific lackeys of the ruling classes, who utilize them for the purpose of concealing the real contradictions which beset a class society. This is done by presenting these contradictions as inner conflicts, by reducing social contradictions to the contradictory nature of the human soul. . . . In the contradictory nature of our thoughts, ideas as well as feelings, materialist psychologists must see the objectively existing contradictions of nature and social life, which are reflected in our thoughts, ideas and feelings." E. T. Chernakov, "Against Idealism and Metaphysics in Psychology," as translated and published in Joseph Wortis, *Soviet Psychiatry* (Baltimore, The Williams & Wilkins Company, 1950), pp. 283-284.

6. As an American apologist for Communism puts it: ". . . materialism cannot conceive and does not accept a concept of mind which blocks off any large segment from interaction with reality. Hence the strenuous objection to the concept of the Freudian unconscious, to the instinct theory, to mental telepathy, or to any other concept of mind which endows it with qualities not derived from material reality. Even the mistaken thoughts of misguided people, from this point of view, are reflections of the material reality of press propaganda, of selfish class influences, of scientific reaction, or represent unwarranted ex-

tensions of special or peculiar experiences. But since mistaken thoughts do not accord with reality, conflicts in the mind of men result, which are often supported by contending social forces: the forces of life and of enlightenment versus the forces of reaction and obscurantism. These in turn are reflections of class forces, so that the force of the progressive working class, its ideology, point of view, scale of values, and its culture emerge as the only true, appropriate and useful system of ideas in the present period. For these reasons political insights and a solid class orientation are regarded as indispensable prerequisites to a realistic approach to life, to a sound social integration or to wholesome psychological development." Joseph Wortis, *Soviet Psychiatry*, p. 71.

7. There are multitudinous instances of this kind of Communist approach to personal life in the autobiographical and descriptive literature on Communism. Among many others, the interested reader will find the following passages at once illuminating and terrifying: Elinor Lipper, *Eleven Years in Soviet Prison Camps* (Chicago, Henry Regnery Co., 1951), pp. 49 ff.; Stephen Spender in *The God That Failed*, ed., Richard Crossman (New York, Harper & Brothers, 1949), pp. 239-241; Wolfgang Leonhard, *Child of the Revolution* (Chicago, Henry Regnery Co., 1958), p. 51; Tamas Aczel and Tibor Meray, *The Revolt of the Mind* (New York, Frederick A. Praeger, 1959), p. 263; Benjamin Gitlow, *I Confess* (New York, E. P. Dutton & Co., 1940), p. 298; Bob Darke, *Cockney Communist* (New York, The John Day Co., 1953), p. 14. For the flavor of matter-of-fact subordination of the personal to the political, however, I know nothing better than a sentence in Charlotte Haldane's description of the opposition of the Party, on political grounds, to her divorce from J. B. S. Haldane. She quotes William Rust of the Political Bureau of the Communist Party of Great Britain: "You can take the question up with the Politburo if you like. . . . I'm sure they will confirm my line." Charlotte Haldane, *Truth Will Out* (New York, Vanguard Press, 1950), p. 177.

8. "Soviet psychology and bourgeois psychology oppose each other in this respect: bourgeois psychology takes the 'unconscious' as a point of departure, as though it were the basic determinant of human psychology, and as though it were the central core of man's personality. Soviet psychology has explicitly fostered

the theory that consciousness is the highest, most specialized human level of development of the psyche and has indicated the dominant role which conscious influences play as compared with unconscious influences. In this regard Soviet psychology is in accord with Soviet pedagogy. Soviet pedagogy maintains as the basic principle of didactics the doctrine of conscious instruction. And, in questions of training, it holds to the principle that it is the conscious personality of man, his conscious behavior, and his conscious discipline that are to be molded." A. P. Fomichev, The Tenth Anniversary of the Resolution of the Central Committee of the All-Union Communist Party (Bolshevik), "Concerning the pedological distortions in the system of the Peoples Commissariat of Education," as quoted in Joseph Wortis, *Soviet Psychiatry*, pp. 119-120.

CHAPTER SIX: RECRUITS

1. Cf.: "It is not the presence of poverty which is new. The new factor in the situation is the presence of millions of modern pagans. Communism is the child of unbelief. Bad social conditions are only the things on which it feeds. . . . I would say that the majority who come to communism do so because, in the first instance, they are subconsciously looking for a cause that will fill the void left by unbelief, or, as in my own case, an insecurely held belief that is failing to satisfy them intellectually and spiritually." Douglas Hyde, *I Believed*, p. 299.

"It would seem that People's Liberation Communism is intimately related to a general process now going on in most underdeveloped areas of the world. Large numbers of people are losing their sense of identity with their traditional ways of life and are seeking restlessly to realize a modern way. . . . They are the people who feel isolated from, and even hostile toward, the ways of their forefathers. But they are also the people who find that as yet they are not personally a part of the new; they are anxious to belong to the future, but they are concerned lest it pass them by." Lucian W. Pye, *Guerrilla Communism in Malaya* (Princeton, N. J., Princeton University Press, 1956), p. 7.

"The fact that communist propaganda is making much more headway among the bourgeoisie and prosperous groups, such as administrators, educators and scientists, than among the peasantry and the working class lends support to the thesis that it is not poverty or even starvation that primarily predisposes men to the attraction of communism. While economic factors undoubtedly play a part, the basic motivations are psychological and emotional. It is the psychological and emotional void created by the loosening of the hold of the traditional religions of India that provides room for what is essentially a new religion of materialism. It is the literate middle-class man so affected who utilises and exploits the economic conditions of the rural and urban toilers." M. R. Masani, *The Communist Party of India* (New York, The Macmillan Co., 1954), p. 237.

". . . people become Communists, for the most part, because of something they find *within* the Communist movement, i.e., in actual *participation* in that movement . . . people tend to seek that something within the Communist movement because, or rather in so far as, they do *not* find it in the political communities to which they belong . . . [whose] characteristic . . . is their *purposelessness,* i.e., their failure to make *demands* upon their members, i.e., their inability to infuse *meaning* into their members' lives. . . ." (Italics in original.) Willmoore Kendall, Introduction to A. Rossi, *A Communist Party in Action* (New Haven, Yale University Press, 1949), p. xviii.

2. This last may seem far-fetched, but one of the outstanding leaders of the Communist Party once told me that when he was a milk-driver with no interests beyond limited and personal ones, it was the pure accident of picking up a leaflet one day which started him on the road to Communism.

3. "As a church, the [Communist] conspiracy attracts the religious natures; as order, it attracts average men; as a war, it attracts the warlike. Each man is caught in a trap for which his own imagination supplies the bait, and they all find in the conspiracy what they themselves have brought to it." Jules Monnerot, *Sociology and Psychology of Communism*, p. 158.

4. *Recruit,* a Communist Party brochure for members, no date, but by internal evidence, 1947.

5. "Remember—every recruit is an individual campaign! You must hand-tailor your approach to the particular person you are trying to recruit. . . . Every prospective recruit has certain special problems. He requires an individual campaign. There-

fore, once your general survey has been made, plan a special approach for each person. Select those phases of the Party's program which would most likely appeal to that particular individual." (*Recruit,* Party brochure.)

6. "One has to be potentially good or intelligent even to be aware that it is not enough simply to drift along without sense of purpose or direction, with neither faith nor ideal. That is why communism so often claims the best, those who feel the miss" (p. 299). ". . . At all costs I must hold fast to what I felt to be the facts, those which I knew from my own experience to be true, the belief that the most evil thing in communism is that it claims some of the best and molds their minds and twists their consciences so that they can be used for the worst" (p. 303). Douglas Hyde, *I Believed.*

CHAPTER SEVEN: THE RANK AND FILE

1. Benjamin Gitlow gives 85 per cent as the figure for the years of his experience, 1919-1929. *I Confess,* p. 291.
   "In the numerically largest European party of the Comintern—the German—these membership fluctuations were intensified during the years of the depression. In 1930, for instance, the German Communist party gained 143,000 new and lost 95,000 old members. The membership of the French Communist party changed in similar fashion. Between 1924 and 1929 it decreased from 68,000 to 46,000. In 1933 it lost nine-tenths of its old members and during the following years up to 1939 gained more than 200,000 members." Ypsilon, *Pattern for World Revolution* (Chicago, Ziff-Davis Publishing Co., 1947), p. 383.
   "The membership of the communist parties was subject to an almost incredible amount of 'fluctuation,' about which complaints abound." This is followed by figures for the German, Czechoslovak, French, British, and American Parties, which are generally confirmatory of this analysis. F. Borkenau, *World Communism* (New York, W. W. Norton & Co., 1939), pp. 366-370.

2. "But there would appear to be a further basic object and result of this technique of secret membership of the Communist Party organized in secret 'cells' or study-groups.

"This object is to accustom the young Canadian adherent gradually to an atmosphere and an ethic of conspiracy. The general effect on the young man or woman over a period of time of *secret* meetings, *secret* acquaintances, and *secret* objectives, plans and policies, can easily be imagined. The technique seems calculated to develop the psychology of a double life and double standards.

"To judge from much of the evidence, the secret adherent is apparently encouraged never to be honest or frank, outside of the secret 'cell' meetings, about his real political attitudes or views, and apparently is led to believe that frankness in these matters is the equivalent of dangerous indiscretion and a potential menace to the organization as a whole. . . .

"An inevitable result of this emphasis on a conspiratorial atmosphere and behaviour even in political discussions, correspondence, and meetings which are in themselves perfectly legal and indeed are the cherished right of everyone in a democratic society, would seem to be the gradual disintegration of normal moral principles such as frankness, honesty, integrity, and a respect for the sanctity of oaths." *Report of the Royal Commission*, pp. 70-71; ital. in original.

3. ". . . le communisme est devenu une *societas perfecta,* avec ses principes, sa hiérarchie, sa structure, ses moeurs, une société vivant au sein de l'autre société qu'il est appelé à renverser et à transformer. Le vrai communiste se sent déjà 'citoyen' d'une autre cité, dont il accepte les lois, en attendant de pouvoir les imposer à tous les autres, le parti est pour lui la préfiguration de la société nouvelle. . . ." A. Rossi, *Physiologie du Parti Communiste Français,* pp. 302-303.

4. "Not only our thinking, but also our vocabulary was reconditioned. Certain words were taboo—for instance, 'lesser evil' or 'spontaneous'. . . . Other words and turns of phrase became favorite stock-in-trade . . . like 'concrete' or 'sectarian'. . . . According to their vocabulary and favorite clichés, you could smell out at once people with Trotskyite, Reformist, Brandlerite, Blanquist and other deviations. And vice versa, Communists betrayed themselves by their vocabulary to the police, and later to the Gestapo. I know of one girl whom the Gestapo had picked up almost at random, without any evidence against her, and

who was caught out on the word 'concrete.' The Gestapo Commissar had listened to her with boredom, half-convinced that his underlings had blundered in arresting her—until she used the fatal word for the second time." Arthur Koestler in *The God That Failed*, pp. 45-46.

5. J. Peters, *The Communist Party—A Manual on Organization*. Reprinted in *Hearings*, Appendix, Part I, U.S. House Special Committee on Un-American Activities, 76th Cong., 1st sess., Washington, 1940, p. 731.

6. "My spare time was the Party's, my home, my income, my happiness and that of my family, were placed in pawn to the Party. And if ever I grew impatient with this, why the Revolution was around the corner, wasn't it?" Bob Darke, *Cockney Communist*, p. 14.

7. "If one is present at the meeting of the secretariat [of the Comintern] and utters an opinion divergent from that of Dimitrov and Manuilsky, he will be listened to. But the decision proposed by the two last-named will be adopted without discussion. There is no voting, only a summary by Dimitrov or Manuilsky." Delgado, *J'ai perdu la foi à Moscou*, p. 115, as cited in David J. Dallin, *The New Soviet Empire*, p. 165.

8. "La 'question éducative' prend . . . la moitié ou le tiers du temps fixé pour la réunion, ce qui confirme l'importance qu'on lui attribue. La nature de ce travail est déterminée par les buts qu'il se propose, qui est celui de 'comprendre la tactique et la politique du parti,' c'est-à-dire le sens et la continuité de cette politique à travers les fluctuations de la tactique. . . ." A. Rossi, *Physiologie du Parti Communiste Français*, p. 301; emphasis in original.

9. "I sat dumbfounded. I had never known anything like it before. What made it worse was the complete calm with which everything was conducted; the pauses in which not a word was spoken, while the nightmare atmosphere in the room never lifted for a second. . . .

"Today, when I look back on this first evening of criticism and self-criticism, I no longer find any difficulty in understanding the system. Every kind of remark—innocent, trivial, completely non-political—was exaggerated and distorted on a gigantic scale, so as to reveal peculiarities of character and political notions. Then these political notions, which one had never formulated, were equated with political actions which one had never committed, and so finally the monstrous consequences were brought to light." Wolfgang Leonhard, *Child of the Revolution* (Chicago, Henry Regnery Co., 1958), pp. 199-201.

10. An illustration of the attitude towards external activities is a question which comes up frequently in Party schools: "Do the workers gain more from losing a strike or from winning it?" The "correct" answer is that in most cases they gain more from winning it. The rationale of the answer is irrelevant here, but the fact that such a question could be raised is highly significant. In the argument the advantages to the workers of winning are never touched upon, but only the question of whether it raises the level of their consciousness, that is, brings them to a more revolutionary position. The Party has no intrinsic interest in the objects of activities in which it engages. It may or may not consider the achievement of these avowed objects desirable or possible, but its real interest is in the value of the activities as a revolutionary proving-ground.
    Cf.: "At first I did not understand the slogan . . . : 'Every defeat is a victory.' Loss of salary, or position, or even loss of life was not important so long as it brought the worker to acceptance of the class struggle." Bella V. Dodd, *School of Darkness* (New York, P. J. Kenedy & Sons, 1954), p. 80.

11. ". . . the basic cause for our paralysis . . . was the true believer's insurmountable horror of excommunication. Though we trusted each other, we shrank from actually giving voice to our heretical thoughts. A shrug, a silence, were the limits to which we could go without outlawing ourselves before our own conscience . . ." (p. 245).
    "I went home alone. While I was waiting for the train in the metro station at St. Germain des Prés, a group of my comrades who had attended the meeting came down the staircase. They walked past to the other end of the platform without a glance, as if I were the invisible man.
    "That journey home in the metro was a foretaste of months and years of loneliness to come. It was not a physical loneliness, for after the break with the Party I found more friends than I have had before. But individual friendships could never replace

the knowledge that one belonged to an international brother-hood embracing the whole globe; nor the warming, reassuring feeling of a collective solidarity which gave to that huge, amorphous mass the coherence and intimacy of a small family" (p. 388). Arthur Koestler, *The Invisible Writing* (New York, The Macmillan Co., 1954).

12. I state the clash between the pre-Communist and Communist ethos in Western terms. The developed Chinese or Indian or Islamic Communist, I know from personal experience as from study, has the same qualities as the developed Communist in the West. Although the ethos with which he grew up differs from the Western ethos—is Confucian or Buddhist or Hindu or Moslem in its inspiration rather than Christian—the fact of the clash remains. The particular form it takes is all that differs.

13. Kant's *Critique of Practical Reason and Other Works on the Theory of Ethics*, "Fundamental Principles of the Metaphysic of Morals" (London, Longmans, Green & Co., 1948), p. 47.

CHAPTER EIGHT: THE CADRE

1. "Every Communist must sacrifice his conscience, his natural moral feelings, to the . . . ideal. What would become of a believer in Moloch who lost his faith in his idol after sacrificing his only beloved son to it?" F. Beck and W. Godin, *Russian Purge and the Extraction of Confession* (New York, Viking Press, 1951), p. 209.

2. "The Party . . . belongs to a psychological order which cannot be confined to any particular manifestation. The relation be-tween such manifestations and the Party is analogous to that between a man and his action. This real psychological being really lives in the real lives of its component individuals, but it cannot be reduced to them. There is *participation* between the Party and the secular religion; and the Party *is* the continually developing realisation of the religion. When vows of world conquest are made to the Party, when men sacrifice to it their enemies or their friends or themselves, it is all dedicated to the secular religion; but it is only we, as outside observers, who make this analytic distinction. The religion is immanent in the Party, and the Party in the religion; and one can see that in

such a situation politics will come to partake of the sacred. The very purpose of the Party is totalitarian, and religion is the only known historical framework that can embrace the sum total of human activities.

"For its members, the Party takes the place both of civilisation and of society (though there are conflicts and the Party's supremacy is not unchallenged); and it is the secular religion (the Party) which provides the model, or pattern, to be conformed to." Jules Monnerot, *Sociology and Psychology of Communism*, pp. 144-145; emphasis in original.

3. "Biszku, who is today Minister of the Interior [of Hungary], was ordered by the Central Committee to speak at the meeting [of rebellious writers just before the Hungarian Revolution of 1956]. He visited Kadar and explained to him that he was unable to obey the order because he was unreservedly on the side of the writers and therefore thought that the best course for him would be to go on a trip or to report sick. Kadar, who also agreed with the writers, remained true to his former—and subsequent—self. 'True,' he told Biszku, 'the writers are right. Yet you cannot disobey the Party.' After a long argument, he persuaded Biszku to speak at the meeting and, out of 'Party discipline,' to make one of the most inciting addresses." Tamas Aczel and Tibor Meray, *The Revolt of the Mind*, footnote, pp. 364-365.

4. This is most strikingly illustrated in the confessions of the "rightists" before the 1957 Session of the National People's Congress of China, as published in *Current Background*, No. 470, July 26, 1957, by the American Consulate General, Hong Kong.

5. "Their [Communists'] primary allegiance was to a revolutionary faith and a vision of man and his material destiny which was given political force by international Communism, of which the American Communist Party and the Russian Communist Party (and hence the Soviet Government, which is only an administrative apparatus of the Russian Communist Party) are component sections." Whittaker Chambers, *Witness*, p. 33.

6. "Adhérer au parti communiste, [c'est] faire le choix d'une destinée. . . . Dans l'adhésion du parti, il y a ce que Paul Nizan appelle la 'coincidence d'une politique et d'un destin.' De sorte que rompre avec le parti, ce n'est point seulement changer

d'étiquette et de classement politiques, c'est recommencer à reconstruire sur de nouveaux plans le monde et soi-même." A. Rossi, *Physiologie du Parti Communiste Français*, p. 338.

7. "The Communist who suffers this singular experience then says to himself: 'What is happening to me? I must be sick.' If he does not instantly stifle that scrap of soul, he is lost. If he admits it for a moment, he had admitted that there is something greater than Reason, greater than the logic of mind, of politics, of history, of economics, which alone justifies the vision. If the party senses his weakness, and the party is peculiarly cunning at sensing such weakness, it will humiliate him, degrade him, condemn him, expel him. If it can, it will destroy him. And the party will be right. For he has betrayed that which alone justifies its faith—the vision of Almighty Man. He has brushed the only vision that has force against the vision of Almighty Mind. He stands before the fact of God.

"The Communist Party is familiar with this experience to which its members are sometimes liable in prison, in illness, in indecision. It is recognized frankly as a sickness. There are ways of treating it—if it is confessed. It is when it is not confessed that the party, sensing a subtle crisis, turns upon it savagely. What ex-Communist has not suffered this experience in one form or another, to one degree or another? What he does about it depends on the individual man. That is why no ex-Communist dare answer for his sad fraternity the question: Why do men break with Communism? He can only answer the question: How did you break with Communism? My answer is: Slowly, reluctantly, in agony." Whittaker Chambers, *Witness*, p. 15.

8. "You will ask: Why, then, do men cease to be Communists? One answer is: Very few do. Thirty years after the Russian Revolution, after the known atrocities, the purges, the revelations, the jolting zigzags of Communist politics, there is only a handful of ex-Communists in the whole world. By ex-Communists I do not mean those who break with Communism over differences of strategy and tactics (like Trotsky) or organization (like Tito). Those are merely quarrels over a road map by people all of whom are in a hurry to get to the same place.

"Nor, by ex-Communists, do I mean those thousands who continually drift into the Communist Party and out again. The turnover is vast. These are the spiritual vagrants of our time whose traditional faith has been leached out in the bland climate of rationalism. They are looking for an intellectual night's lodging. They lack the character for Communist faith because they lack the character for any faith. So they drop away, though Communism keeps its hold on them.

"By an ex-Communist, I mean a man who knew clearly why he became a Communist, who served Communism devotedly and knew why he served it, who broke with Communism unconditionally and knew why he broke with it. Of these there are very few—an index of the power of the vision and the power of the crisis." Whittaker Chambers, *Witness*, p. 12.

9. There are scattered indications, both in the memoirs of ex-Communists and in one or two novels, such as Manès Sperber's trilogy (*The Burned Bramble; The Abyss; Journey without End*), which tend to confirm my analysis and do not at any point contradict it. The only deeply analytical examination of the process as a whole of which I know is in Whittaker Chambers' *Witness* (a part of which is reproduced in Notes 7 and 8 above), and that also confirms my conclusions.

CHAPTER NINE: PARTY TRAINING SCHOOLS

1. The literature on Communism is full of testimony to the existence of multifarious schools for all levels and all specialized sections of the cadre.

For example, for France: "Once the cadres have been selected, it is necessary to train them. For this there are 'cadre schools'. . . . From the beginning of 1947 to the middle of 1948 three schools with four-month training periods operated to train national officers. During the same period, eleven schools with four-week training periods were created for Communist militants in the trade union movement, in peasant organizations, in women's groups, and in youth movements. At the federation level, 129 schools, in session for two weeks, assembled 2,071 leaders of federal and section committees. In the first six months of 1948, 6,344 militants took courses in 777 schools. We must add many study centers intended for members of parliament, editors of newspapers, and others." Mario Einaudi,

Jean-Marie Domenach, and Aldo Garosci, *Communism in Western Europe*, pp. 94-95.

For Italy: "To pass a three or a six months' course of ideological specialization [at *L'Istituto di Studi Comunisti*] is the dream of all the 340,000 young Communists who have frequented the lower party schools of different degrees all over Italy during the past years. . . . Among the . . . Party schools of a lower level, the most important are above all a special centre in Bologna for male students from parts of Italy where Communism still is not strong and a special centre for women— accommodation for sixty—in Como near the Swiss border, and then the ordinary district schools in all the reddest parts of Italy or in Emilia, Lombardy, Tuscany, Piedmont and Liguria and the so-called provincial schools in Ravenna, Bologna, Reggio Emilia, Perrara, Siena, Arezzo, Milan, Udine and Florence." Gunnar Kumlien, "A Letter from Rome," *The Tablet* [London], February 5, 1955, p. 130.

See also: Aczel and Meray, *The Revolt of the Mind,* pp. 46-47 (Hungary); Leonhard, *Child of the Revolution,* pp. 177-179 (Comintern school), pp. 365-367, 372 (Germany); Einaudi, Domenach, and Garosci, *Communism in Western Europe*, p. 204 (Italy); North, *Moscow and Chinese Communists,* pp. 197-198, 260-262 (China); Justus M. van der Kroef, "Indonesian Communism under Aidit," *Problems of Communism,* Nov.-Dec., 1958, p. 16, footnote 4; Heinrich von Einsiedel, *I Joined the Russians* (New Haven, Yale University Press, 1953), Chap. 7 (Soviet Union); El Campesino, *Life and Death in Soviet Russia* (New York, G. P. Putnam's Sons, 1952), Chap. 6; Fischer, *Stalin and German Communism,* pp. 509-510 (The Lenin School); Krivitsky, *In Stalin's Secret Service,* pp. 58-59 (Comintern schools).

Testimony before the House Committee on Un-American Activities and the Senate Internal Security Subcommittee has revealed the existence of a whole network of schools at the highest level for foreign Communists in the Soviet Union. Where, in the decades before the war, the Lenin School, the University of the Peoples of the East, and one or two specialized institutions comprised the top echelon of institutions for the training of the cadre of the various Parties, today there seems to be an indefinite number of schools at the disposal of the foreign sec-

tion of the Central Committee of the Communist Party of the
Soviet Union.

2. Cf.: "Of all the Party schools, this one on Karolina Avenue
was the most important. . . . The students came from every
corner of the country. There were Party secretaries of the
various Budapest iron works, the commander of the southern
frontier guards, agitation-propaganda personnel from the min-
ing district, the working-class director of a textile factory, the
chairman of the best village cooperative, a university lecturer,
the headmaster of a country school, the head of a village coun-
cil, and workaday members of the Party machinery." Tamas
Aczel and Tibor Meray, *The Revolt of the Mind*, pp. 47-48.

3. Relaxation in the schools is indeed a very serious political
matter. Although I know this to be the case, I would hardly
expect my readers to believe me unless I had confirmation
from Wolfgang Leonhard's report on the Comintern School he
attended in the Soviet Union: "Our working time was so full
up that the only free time we had was on Saturday afternoon
and Sunday. . . . It was clear, however, that the school authorities recognised that a little gaiety and relaxation was needed,
and a resolution was passed to this effect. The immediate result
was a meeting of the group to discuss the theme of 'relaxation' [!]. Klassner gave us an address. . . . 'It is of the highest
importance that we should meet together sometimes outside
working hours'. . . . The result was a model of the realisation
of theory in practice. . . . We sang in the grave and disciplined
manner which was expected of us in everything, but on this
occasion it did not seem right. We received a new directive
from Wandel: 'Comrades, you must sing more gaily and cheer-
fully.' " *Child of the Revolution*, pp. 194-195.

4. " 'Look into yourself' . . . 'discover the roots' . . . 'kill the
petty-bourgeois remnants in yourself. . . .' How often the writer
had to listen to these warnings during his period at the school!
Then the headmaster presented the question to the study group,
and the fellow students—to help him, naturally—'evaluated'
his entire attitude. For hours they discussed him, pulled him
to pieces, argued about him, and, in the end, it invariably
turned out that, 'although he is a good guy, a decent comrade,
he couldn't *quite* fit into the collective.' The working-class
woman whom, for long months, *he* had helped with her work,

said that he had helped her too much, thus preventing her from working independently. The reason for it—she said—was quite obvious: he undervalued the capabilities of the working class. The army officer declared that, whenever the school marched together in demonstrations, he had noticed that the writer never sang with the others. This, beyond a doubt, was caused by some petty-bourgeois bashfulness. . . . Naturally, such 'individual evaluations' were not restricted to writers. Every student of the Party school had his turn. Some of them were so badly 'manhandled' by their fellow students that they walked around in a daze for weeks. There were innumerable such cases of mild nervous breakdowns." Tamas Aczel and Tibor Meray, *The Revolt of the Mind*, pp. 51-52; emphasis in original.

"The students became terribly upset and very unhappy during this period [intensive self-criticism program]. Girls often broke into tears, weeping aloud under this constant probing into their thoughts and the internal struggles brought about in their mental systems. But they weren't the only ones to collapse. Men did also. They wept more than the girls, it seemed, but they were under greater pressure. Girls had fewer social contacts, politically speaking, and so comparatively less pressure was put on them. Some tried to escape from what seemed an insoluble problem by leaping into the quietude of Kwan Ming Lake within the grounds of the Summer Palace. Some tried other ways of committing suicide." Edward Hunter, *Brainwashing in Red China*, p. 38.

"Every one of us has to tell his life story and examine his social and political attitude in front of his comrades. The others are supposed to criticize what is said in order to help one 'discover one's weaknesses.' " Einsiedel, *I Joined the Russians*, p. 166.

5. Cf.: Leonhard, *Child of the Revolution*, pp. 184, 369; Aczel and Meray, *The Revolt of the Mind*, p. 48; Hunter, *Brainwashing in Red China*, pp. 26-27.

6. For two excellent concrete examples of teaching in cadre schools, see Leonhard, *Child of the Revolution*, pp. 209-213; Aczel and Meray, *The Revolt of the Mind*, pp. 49-51.

INDEX

Activity, 93, 111; of rank and filers, 122-25; as training maneuvers, 123-24; as necessary to develop basic qualities, 124-25

Aczel, Tamas, 196 n7, 204 n3, 207 n1, 208 n2, 4, 209 n5, 6

Adlerian typology, 92

Agitation: definition of, 94; and propaganda, 93-95

Alienation, 75-78

Almond, Gabriel, 178 n4

Anti-Dühring, 40

"Anti-Party" attitudes, 81-82, 138

Augustine, 73

Bauer, Raymond A., 189 n1

Beck, F., 203 n1

Bell, Daniel, 182 n25, 183 n2

Bolshevik: as honorific title, 11; "tired bolshevik," 41. *See also* Cadre

Bolshevization, 94, 139, 142

Borkenau, F., 199 n1

Brandt, Conrad, 179 n6, 185 n9, 191 n9

Break with the Party, 12, 155-58

Brecht, Bertolt, 25, 182 n23, 192 n11

Browder, Earl, 143

Browder, Robert Paul, 190 n2

Bruckberger, J. L., 180 n9

Cadre: definition of, 14; criteria for, 17-24; transition to, 20, 142-43; training in daily life of, 144; self-criticism, 152-53; subjectivity, 153; objectivity, 153-55

—Characteristics: ideal Communist, 16; quasi-priestly caste, 16; "people of special mould," 17; tone of cadre Communist, 144, 148, 151; Party as necessary condition for significant existence, 145, 154; iron discipline and independent initiative, 146-52; internal conflicts, 146-52, 154; quality of loyalty, 149

—Crisis, 133-42; Party-engineered, 137-41

—Role: relation to Party as a whole, 13; as elite, 13-14; as soul of Party and "vanguard of proletariat," 14; identification of, 15; position in Party, 15; relationship to formal leadership, 15; relation to espionage, underground work, 15

—Schools: universal character of, 161; guiding principles of, 161-62; selection of students, 162-63; function of, 163-65; organization of, 164-65; curriculum of, 165-68

Cahiers du Communisme, 32

Calomiris, Angela, 186 n*11*

Campesino, El, 207 n*1*

Capital, 40

Capitalist production, 64-65

Carew Hunt, R. N., 191 n*5*, 191 n*9*

Castro, Fidel, 70

Chambers, Whittaker, 157, 182n*22*, 194 n*23*, 204 n*5*, 205 n*7, 8*, 206 n*9*

Chernakov, E. T., 195 n*5*

Communist, The, 33

Communist consciousness, 4, 49, 51, 52, 77, 85

Communist ethos: clash with Western ethos, 130, 133

Communist "hardening," 142

Communist Manifesto, 40

Communist Party. *See* Party, the

Communists: sense of separation from others, 129-30

Communist will. *See* Will

Conscious control. *See* Control

Conscious mind. *See* Communist consciousness

Consciousness: political consciousness, 52, 62; "trade-union consciousness," 52, 61. *See also* Communist consciousness

Conspiratorial attitudes, 122

Conspiratorial techniques: role of, 106

Contact with the masses, 23

Control: conscious control, 18; as "scientific," 38; existence regarded as, 39; life and thought as, 54-55

Criticism and self-criticism. *See* Self-criticism

Critique of the Gotha Program, 40

Crossman, Richard, 189 n*13*, 196 n7

Current Background, 204 n*4*

Cynicism, 24-26

Daily Worker, 128

Dallin, David J., 190 n*2*, 201 n*7*

Darke, Bob, 179 n*8*, 184 n*8*, 186 n*11*, 196 n*7*, 201 n*6*

Delgado, 201 n7

Democratic centralism, 109

Developed Communist. *See* Cadre

Devotion to the Party: as control, 17-18. *See also* Party, devotion to

Dialectical materialism, 53, 166

Dictatorship of the proletariat, 68

Discipline, 20, 21

Discourse on Method, 40

Dmitrov, 9, 17, 19, 20, 23, 25, 143, 177 n*1*, 180 n*11, 13, 14, 15*, 181 n*19*, 182 n*24*

Dodd, Bella V., 202 n*10*

Domenach, Jean-Marie, 178 n*5*, 206 n*1*, 207 n*1*

Economic theory, 63-66

Education: New Members' Classes, 111-13; the unit "educational," 118-19; inner schools, 159; rank-and-file schools and classes, 160-61; cadre schools, 161-69

Einaudi, Mario, 178 n*5*, 206 n*1*, 207 n*1*

Einsiedel, Heinrich von, 207 n*1*, 209 n*4*

Emotions: Party attitude toward, 46, 47, 80-84; as subjective problems, 73; as "personal problems," 80

Engels, 167, 193 n*12, 13*, 194 n*2, 3*

Essay concerning Human Understanding, 40

Fainsod, Merle, 186 n*11*

Fairbank, John K., 179 n*6*, 185 n*9*, 191 n*9*

Fischer, Ruth, 182 n23, 192 n11, 207 n1

Flexibility, 22

Flynn, Elizabeth Gurley, 128

Fomichev, A. P., 196 n8

"Formulation," 150-51

Foundations of Leninism, 40

Freedom: as experienced by Communist, 16, 21, 76, 113, 119; as recognition of necessity, 57

Freud, 73, 74

Freudian typology, 92

Fromm, 74

Garosci, Aldo, 178 n5, 206 n1, 207 n1

General crisis of capitalism, 65

German Ideology, 40

Gitlow, Benjamin, 186 n11, 196 n7, 199 n1

Godin, 203 n1

Haldane, Charlotte, 196 n7

Hard-core Communists, 4, 10. See also Cadre

Hegel, 16, 75

Historical materialism, 58-61

History: as incarnate, 16, 21, 24, 64, 68, 71, 126

History of the Communist Party of the Soviet Union, 18, 180 n12, 181 n20, 193 n18

Hunter, Edward, 185 n10, 209 n4, 5

Hyde, Douglas, 178 n5, 185 n10, 197 n1, 199 n6

Ideal type of Communist, 10-13, 16-26

Idealism, 24-26

Imperialism, 40

Imperialism: Leninist theory of, 65

Independence of judgment, 20-21

Initiative, 20

Institutes, 40

Intellect: role of, 45, 46

Invincibility: feeling of, 60-61, 66, 126

Joining the Party: decision of large proportions, 103

Judgment: one primordial judgment, 46

Jung, 73, 74

Jungian typology, 92

Kant, 130, 203 n13

Kautsky, 193 n16

Kendall, Willmoore, 198 n1

Khrushchev, 50, 51, 155

Kintner, William R., 181 n17

Koestler, Arthur, 180 n9, 181 n16, 184 n7, 186 n13, 192 n11, 200 n4, 202 n11

Krivitsky, W. G., 207 n1

Kumlien, Gunnar, 207 n1

Labedz, Leopold, 190 n3

"Left Wing" Communism, 40

Leites, Nathan, 194 n1

Lenin, 4, 9, 16, 33, 50, 52, 56, 65, 67, 167, 181 n18, 183 n5, 191 n7, 192 n10, 193 n16, 17

Leonhard, Wolfgang, 196 n7, 201 n9, 207 n1, 208 n3, 209 n4, 5, 6

Leviathan, 40

Lipper, Elinor, 196 n7

Liu Shao-ch'i, 194 n4

Malenkov, 50

Mao Tse-tung, 167, 179 n6, 185 n9, 191 n9

Marx, Karl, 34, 64, 65, 67, 75, 167, 191 n8, 193 n13, 14, 15, 194 n2, 3

Marxist-Leninist classics, 40

Masani, M. R., 198 n1

Mass Parties: as "transmission belts," 14

Massey, 143
Materialism and Empirio-Criticism, 40
Meray, Tibor, 196 n7, 204 n3, 207 n1, 208 n2, 4, 209 n5, 6
Milosz, Czeslaw, 183 n2, 184 n7
Mindel, "Pop," 32, 47
Monnerot, Jules, 177 n3, 191 n6, 193 n11, 198 n3, 203 n2
Moral theory, 52, 56-58

Nasser, 70
Nehru, 70
Neurosis: Party attitude toward, 80, 82
North, Robert C., 195 n4, 207 n1

Objectivity, 153-55

Party, the: break with, 12, 155-58
—Mystique of the Party: devotion and commitment, 17, 24-25, 62, 126-27, 129-30, 138, 139, 142, 154-55, 158; "The Party is always right," 22, 144-45; materialist sacrament, 24-25, 62, 63, 158, 162; Party line as Truth, 34, 150; theory transforms facts, 66, 155; potential future society, 77, 78; identification with the Party, 119, 120, 132, 135-37, 144, 153-54; identification with the power of the Party, 125-26; "state within a state," 127-28
—Organization: turnover, 105; purges, 105, 138-41; new members, 105-11; induction, 107-11; financial demands, 110-11; demands on time, 111; "checkup," 111, 120; the unit meeting, 114-22; "parliamentary procedure," 115-16; the unit bureau, 117; agenda of unit meetings, 117-18; organizational training,

121-22; unlimited demands, 135; abstention as form of voting, 140; treatment of defectors, 155-56
—Theory of the Party, 61-63: "party of a new type," 62; Party as only highest form of mass organization, 94; mass Party vs. iron Party, 104, 138
—Party training: responsibility for, 27; forms of, 28-31; formal education, role of, 28; in activity, 29; no separation between training and life, 29-31, 32, 37, 125-31; methodology of, 32-38; ideological dredging, 36; utilization of pressure, 40-45; linking of petty to momentous, 43, 108; "fighting for a position," 116
Personality: transformation of, 45-48, 162; theory of, 75-78; crisis of, 133
Personal life: Party regulation of, 127, 128-29
Peters, J., 181 n17, 201 n5
Pieck, Wilhelm, 143
Political economy, 63
Political theory, 66-69
Politics: as war, 68
Pollitt, Harry, 143
Pressure: in life of cadre, 132, 143, 144, 148, 150, 152, 154; as decisive tool of training, 162; in cadre schools, 165
Principe, Il, 40
Problems of Leninism, 40
Professional revolutionaries, 4, 9, 14, 27
Propaganda: definition of, 94
Psychiatry: Party opposition to, 78
Psychological anesthesia of Communists, 18, 39, 53, 74
Psychological types, 11-13, 92

Psychology: reductionist approach to, 78-79
Psychosurgery, 72, 80-85
Pye, Lucian W., 197 n*1*

Rationality, 18, 40, 52-54
Recruiting: objective factors, 90-93; subjective factors, 93-95; problem of, 95-96; techniques of, 96-103; last-minute "blocks," 98; and cadre-potentiality, 101; and strategic usefulness, 101; role of recruiting "quotas," 101-02; and "concentration work," 102
Report of the Royal Commission (Ottawa), 177 n*2*, 199 n*2*
Responsibility: assuming of, 20; to act, 38; attitude of, 120
Revisionism, 123
Riesmanian typology, 92
Rossi, A., 178 n*3*, 179 n*5*, 182 n*1*, 184 n*6*, 186 n*12*, 190 n*2*, 200 n*3*, 201 n*8*, 204 n*6*

Schwartz, Benjamin, 179 n*6*, 185 n*9*, 191 n*9*
"Science" of Marxism-Leninism, 16, 113: as knowledge for control, 38-39
"Scientific" character of reality, 54-55
Self-criticism, 12, 42, 44, 48, 121, 152-53, 165, 168
Self discipline, 144
Self-reversal syndrome, 125, 136-37
Selznick, Philip, 179 n*5*, 181 n*21*
Sex: Party attitude toward, 47, 81
Sheldonian typology, 92
Spender, Stephen, 196 n*7*
Sperber, Manès, 180 n*8*, 206 n*9*
Stalin, 9, 14, 16, 23, 33, 50, 51, 148, 155, 167, 179 n*7*, 180 n*10*, 193 n*19*, *20*, 194 n*21*

Stalinization. *See* Bolshevization
State and Revolution, 40
State, the: as force, 67-68; "withering away" of, 67; theory of, 66-69
Strategy and tactics, 69-71: as concern of every Communist, 70
Subjectivity, 12, 80, 82, 120-21, 135, 153
Sukarno, 70
Summa, 40
Surplus value, 64

Tactics, 69-71
Theory: as mode of the personality, 19; as consciously held, 49; as limiting, 50; stress on, 50-52, 62, 118-19; conditioning factors, 51; economic, 63-66; as belief, 66; as transforming facts, 66. *See also* Unity of theory and practice
Thorez, Maurice, 143
Triska, Jan F., 194 n*22*
Two Tactics, 40

Ulam, Adam B., 190 n*4*
Ulbricht, Walter, 143
Unconscious, the, 72, 73, 85
Unity of theory and practice, 20, 21, 23, 32, 37, 39, 54-55, 58, 62, 69, 162

Value, 64
van der Kroef, Justus M., 207 n*1*

What Is To Be Done?, 40, 52
Will, 16, 25-26, 45-46, 135-37, 154, 155, 158
Wortis, Joseph, 195 n*5, 6*, 196 n*8*
Wright, Richard, 187 n*13*

Ypsilon, 199 n*1*